BURN ZONES

ZONES

PLAYING LIFE'S BAD HANDS

JORGE P. NEWBERY

BURN ZONES
Playing Life's Bad Hands

ISBN 978-1-61961-320-1

Community
Books

Contents

Introduction

WHEN I RACED BICYCLES, I LOOKED AT RACES AS HAVING "burn zones," which were relatively short periods of extraordinary effort that separated the winners and losers. Burn zones could include a long climb or a section with major crosswinds in which those skilled in riding in an echelon formation excelled. Most of the top riders could be in contention for most of the race, but the burn zones would eliminate the majority of racers from contention. The burn zones were not always marked by external physical factors, and could simply be a series of attacks and chases and breakaways, which came in such velocity that those who were not in top shape were left behind. I was very good at training, being focused, and disciplined. *"Stay relaxed,"* I counseled myself when I entered a burn zone. *"Others around you are hurting just as much as you. Focus on enduring the pain until the pace slows. The effort will get easier soon."*

Everyone's life is full of burn zones, which test the limits of our bodies and minds.

I started working when I was seven-years-old and created my first business at 11. I dropped out of high school at 16, as I was eager to learn in the real world. I repeatedly took chances and worked tirelessly to turn my visions into reality. I built a record company, raced bicycles alongside some of the best in the world, and embarked on a real estate crusade to fix the unfixable. I took on our country's most troubled buildings and transformed them into assets to benefit all. Any achievement of consequence was the result of preparing for and enduring burn zones.

Despite financial success, I eschewed any trappings of luxury—instead living a Spartan lifestyle. I rarely ate out and limited my intake of processed food. The majority of my meals emerged from a Crockpot into which brown rice and beans were mixed with whatever vegetables were on sale that week. I took pride in driving any car to 200,000 miles before casting it away. I even clipped coupons, recognizing that—thanks to taxes—the dollar you save is more important than the dollar you earn. I lived with my parents until I was 29, although this would not be considered uncommon in my father's homeland of Argentina. My thrifty approach maximized the dollars I had available to play with in my real-life game of Monopoly, and these lifestyle choices helped ready me for the uphill sprints life could throw my way.

Fueled with cash earned and saved between 1992 and 2004, I amassed over 4,000 apartment units across the United States, resulting in a net worth in the tens of millions. I thought I could surmount any burn zone, but I took one chance too many.

One natural disaster erased everything. An ice storm plunged me into a battle with the elite, those much more powerful than me. In my struggle to survive, I was maligned, publicly shamed, and financially gutted. I lost everything and emerged over $26 million in debt. I had entered the most difficult burn zone of my life.

CHAPTER ONE

Paperboy to Record Mogul

MY FLAWS	MY STRENGTHS
1. I am very optimistic	1. I am very optimistic
2. I defer gratification	2. I defer gratification
3. I tend to see the good in people	3. I tend to see the good in people
4. I like to help people	4. I like to help people
5. I work too hard	5. I work very hard
6. I am too trusting	6. I am very trusting
7. I am very tough on myself	7. I am very tough on myself
8. I take the difficult road	8. I show others the path to the easy road
9. I give the job to the less-experienced but more eager candidate, in hopes that they rise to the occasion	9. I give the job to the less-experienced but more eager candidate, in hopes that they rise to the occasion
10. I do not delegate enough	10. I can work 18 hours a day if needed

"Can I deliver the paper?" I asked, after chasing the newspaper delivery person's car down on my Raleigh Chopper, a bicycle modeled after a motorcycle chopper. I was shy, except when it came to business, and I learned early not to be afraid to ask for what I want. The year was 1973 in Los Angeles.

"How old are you?" asked Robert Snodgrass, the *Herald Examiner*'s district manager, with a look of amusement.

"Seven," I replied. Mr. Snodgrass' brow crinkled.

"You think you can deliver the papers every day, on time?" he asked, sounding skeptical.

"Yes, I can do it," I said, with as much determination as I could muster. I wanted to work. I knew that I could figure out the logistics once the job was mine. Besides, the day was March 1st and I had said "White Rabbits" that morning as soon as I woke up, just like I did on the first of every month. My mother had taught me that this ritual empowered me with good luck.

"And will your parents be alright with this?" he asked, warming up to the idea.

"Sure," I replied. "They will."

A week later, I was zooming the streets of Brentwood Glen on my Chopper, delivering the *Herald* every day. Within a few months, I reasoned that as long as I was riding the streets delivering the *Herald*, I could also efficiently deliver the competing paper, the *Evening Outlook*. Delivering both at the same time

Taking a break from my paper route, around age seven

took about 50% more time, yet I was earning double. Lugging so many papers on the back of my bike was hard work, but there were a few streets north of our house so I would deliver those first, then return to my house and reload the papers to deliver to the streets to the south.

I delivered the papers every afternoon after school during the week and mornings on the weekends. I enjoyed my daily rides through the Glen, although rainy days were challenging. I had to spend extra time to carefully wrap the papers in plastic bags so they would not get wet and toss them gingerly to avoid puddles. Although I would return from my route drenched, my mum always had a reward for me.

"Mum," I'd yell as I walked in the side door to the laundry room, sopping wet. "I'm home." My mum would run me a hot bath. The worst of these stormy days were my first burn zones. A part of me relished these challenging days, as if I was playing level 10 of my paperboy game, with the prize of a hot bath upon my successful completion.

Being a loner, this was real-life play to me and my rewards were my pay. However, the grand prizes came every December when I gave all my customers Christmas cards, which I signed with my home address. My customers would then mail me tips: cash and checks, often $5 or $10, sometimes $20 a shot! After I returned home from my route, I would sit at the dining table and open the envelopes. I was winning at this game.

Although I enjoyed delivering the papers, I did not relish reading them. The stories often recounted horrors of abuse, muggings, and other attacks. The local police blotter scared me the most, as some of the crimes were within miles of my house. As I read, my mind would transport my body into that of the abused and I could sense the agony they suffered. I remember the 1974 story of the live-in managers at the Star Motel in Santa Monica, which is where we went to the beach and only 10 minutes from our house. Someone robbed the couple who were the managers, bound them at the wrists and ankles, then shot them each once in the head and set them on fire. I could comprehend the robbing part as they got the money. However, I couldn't move past the killings. Why didn't they just leave? Why did they have to shoot them dead and set them aflame?

I had trouble comprehending why people would treat others so badly.

PEDALING ICE CREAM

By age 11, I had saved several hundred dollars from my paper routes. I got up the courage to knock on the door of Chris, a teenager on Gladwin Street, which was a block away. Many summers, Chris would ride through our neighborhood selling ice cream off a large tricycle outfitted with a freezer in the front and a bullhorn-type speaker bellowing ice cream truck melodies, all powered by a car battery. The sleek ice cream tricycle had been a neighborhood staple when I was younger—I was a faithful customer—but we hadn't seen Chris out with it for the last couple of summers.

"Hi Chris," I said when he answered the door. He was maybe 17 with long blond hair, a surfer to the hilt. He was wearing blue OP shorts and a yellow Hang Ten imprint T-shirt. "I'm Jorge. I live on Homedale." I held out my hand.

"Hi," Chris said, clearly uncertain as to why I was on his doorstep. He hesitantly shook my hand. We did a regular handshake, like my father did, and though I was years younger than Chris, the gesture seemed foreign to him. I bet Chris usually did the surfer shake, like most of the older kids did, but I wasn't sure how to do it.

"I wanted to know if you still had the ice cream trike," I said. "I used to buy ice cream sandwiches from you all the time." Chris' eyes suddenly warmed.

"I remember you now," he said, now smiling. "You got two older sisters, right?"

"Yes," I said.

"Charlene and..." he started.

"Anne," I replied.

"That's right, Anne," he said. "How are they doing?"

"They're fine," I said. I had noticed that the older boys seemed to take an interest in my sisters.

"Well, follow me," he instructed. I walked in and followed Chris through the house and out the back door into the garage. Chris flipped the light switch on and I saw my future: the trike, albeit a bit worn out with three flat tires.

"How much?" I asked. Chris looked at me.

"How old are you?" he asked.

"Eleven," I said.

"You going to fix this up and start selling ice cream?" he asked, sounding skeptical. His tone reminded me of Mr. Snodgrass when I first asked to deliver the *Herald Examiner.*

"Yes," I said. "I can do it."

"Do you have $300?" he asked.

"The tires are flat and I see some rust," I said. "It looks like it will take a lot of work to get it going again—$300 is too much. How about $150?"

Chris laughed or maybe it was a scoff. I couldn't really distinguish which it was. *"Who does this grommet think he is?"* I imagined him thinking. That's what his puzzled face certainly seemed to be saying. "$250," he finally said. "And that's a bargain." I had $200 in one pocket and $40 in the other, just in case. I had gone to the door wanting to spend $200 and was now in striking distance.

"$200," I said. "I can give you the cash right now."

Chris laughed. This time I was certain it was a laugh. "That's cool," he said. "You got a deal." He extended his hand, this time with the surfer grip. I looked at his hand and back at Chris' face.

"I can do this," I thought. I reached out my hand in my interpretation of a surfer grip: hand high, elbow low, and I looked him straight in the eye. We shook hands awkwardly. "Thanks!"

I said. I wasn't sure how long to hold on, but I think I held on a bit too long. It was clear that this was my first time.

"Let me write you a receipt," Chris said. He pulled his hand back from mine in a jerky motion, which seemed to be telling me *"the handshake's over, little dude."* As he walked away, he looked back and said, "Wait here. I'll be right back."

Once Chris returned, he handwrote a receipt from paper he pulled out of a Pee-Chee folder. I handed over the $200 in mostly small bills. Chris counted them out, signed the receipt, and then handed it over. The trike was mine.

"Thanks Chris," I said. I wanted to try the surfer shake again and started reaching out my hand.

"Tell Charlene and Anne I said hi" said Chris, as he gave me a wave. I quickly converted my extended hand into a wave.

I pushed the trike home and burst through the front door. "Mum, Alastair, Charles!" I yelled as soon as I stepped inside. "I bought the ice cream trike." Soon, they were all in our driveway admiring my first major business acquisition. I felt good. This was a big step for me, and I enjoyed seeing the glimmer in my brain manifest into a real business. Over the next few weekends, I painted and buffed the trike back to glory. I stenciled the letters "George's Ice Cream" and my parents' address on each side of the trike to satisfy health department requirements. Then, I rode the bike about three miles to the West Los Angeles City Hall to obtain business and health department licenses.

My first major business acquisition: the sleek ice cream trike

Soon enough, my summer afternoons included two rounds of every street in my neighborhood, peddling ice cream to my neighbors. I would even take the trike to evening football games at Brentwood School, even though the route included a treacherous stretch up Acari Street, a curvy hill that challenged my legs on the way up and my handling skills on the way down.

Reviewing ads in the *Recycler,* the hard-copy predecessor to Craigslist, I found a large freezer, which I bought to store my ice cream supply. Every Saturday, my father would drive me to the wholesale ice cream outlet in Culver City, which was 10 to 20 minutes from home depending on traffic. We pulled up to the refrigerated warehouse and lined up our Volkswagen Squareback in a queue of ice cream trucks to buy Creamsicles,

Drumsticks, Popsicles, Big Sticks, and, my personal favorite, ice cream sandwiches.

Then came the high-stakes drive home. The key was to make the lights and not get stuck on the long reds. "Dad, please make that light," I said, looking at the flashing "Don't Walk" signal threatening our green light. "We need to get home before everything melts."

"I am driving the speed limit," my father replied. "I don't want to get in an accident or get a ticket over ice cream."

Looking back, I realize I must have driven him crazy on these drives. I was in the shotgun seat, yet acted like a backseat driver. But I had my product to think of! I was a serious operator, not just some kid having fun. If one of my customers found that the round top of a Drumstick flattened due to a melt/refreeze incident, I would always exchange it for another. The defective goody would end up in my family's freezer, where my siblings could devour it (and my profit margin). Keeping the ice cream cold was a higher priority to me than my dad's driving record.

Keeping the treats cold in the tricycle was another matter. Every day, I would ride my 10-speed bike to Barrington Ice to buy a few slabs of dry ice, which I put in my backpack. The dry ice often gave my back a burning sensation as I rode the several miles back home, pedaling fast so I could to take the pack off sooner. All this cycling made my legs strong and turned me into an inadvertent athlete. I started accompanying my father to 10Ks and longer running races on the weekends, where I frequently placed at the top of my age category and even finished ahead of him.

THE SEDUCTIVE PAYCHECKS OF A BUSBOY

"I am here to apply for the busboy job," I said to the older lady with red hair behind the counter at the UCLA Faculty Center. I was 13 and looking to take my professional life to the next level, responding to a Help Wanted ad in the *Evening Outlook*.

"Here's an application," she said, peering over the counter as she handed me the application attached to a clipboard and a pen.

When I finished, I returned the application to the counter. The older lady with red hair got up and quickly scanned it. "Everything appears to be in order," she said. "However, you are only 13. Are you sure you are ready to work?" Her tone reminded me of both Mr. Snodgrass and Chris.

"Yes," I said. "I am a good worker."

"I think you need a work permit from your school," she said.

"I can ask," I replied. "I am not sure." I could tell that she wasn't sure either.

"Are you available to work tonight?" she asked.

"Yes," I said. "How soon?"

"Could you start now?" she asked. "We are short-handed and really need the help."

"Yes," I said. I had just landed my first regular job. Over the next several weeks, I proved myself dependable and hard working. I took on extra hours whenever someone else couldn't make it. The request for a work permit was soon forgotten, which was just as well, as the permit would have limited my hours.

I enjoyed the fun and camaraderie of working with my older, college age co-workers. Steve, or "The Professor," was a nerdy graduate student and we became friends. He was super smart, but socially awkward—kind of like me. Even though I was much younger, I always did more than my share of work, especially since others did not take the work that seriously. I realized this about a week into the job on a night when there were maybe a dozen of us cleaning up after a banquet of over 300. When I was busy bussing dirty dishes off the tables, I got struck.

I took a hit in the back. My lower left side. I heard the thud of the impact. I turned around to view my attacker.

Renee, lean and blond with Farrah Fawcett hair and high cheek-bones, was maybe 30 feet away and grinning ear-to-ear with a dinner roll in her hand. "Roll fight!" she screamed. At that moment, dinner rolls started flying all around the room. I took cover behind my bus cart to survey the situation.

I broke from my crouch and crawled over to the nearest table. A couple of rolls whisked over my head. I was on full alert, my eyes darting around to every one of my co-workers, and my body low to stay out of the line of fire. As I reached the table, I extended my arm gingerly to the dinner roll basket. I felt one, two, three rolls. I pulled the basket down and shimmied back to the cover of the cart. I shot one over at "The Professor," the only employee not participating in the battle. The roll must have caught a draft as it went a bit high and hit him in the back of the head.

"You children," he bellowed, as he swung around, furious. "Get back to work." All of us snapped to work as though nothing had happened. I made myself look busy by picking up dishes. I don't think he suspected that I was the guilty one. As he settled down and turned back around, I scanned the room for my next target. I eyed Renee, who now had her back turned as she busily cleared a table. I pulled my arm back and chucked hard. The roll hit her right in the derriere.

"Who threw that?" she said, turning around while her hand brushed her bottom, acting as if the roll really hurt. Our eyes met. I still had a roll left. I was smiling as I had my prey in sight and she had no protection. I cocked my arm back. Just then, she started smiling slyly, her eyes focused elsewhere behind me. I readied my arm again.

I got hit in the shoulder, then the back. I dropped my roll and instinctively hit the ground. I heard laughter. As I got back up, I saw "The Professor" smiling like I have never seen him smile before, although I guessed that was not saying too much as I had only been there a week.

"Get back to work, scrub," he said.

"Yeah, scrub," I heard Renee say, giggling. I looked over and her ample smile had returned. Work was my play and my social outlet. Plus, the paychecks were seductive: hundreds of dollars every couple of weeks. My parents paid for my food, housing and whatever else I needed, so I saved most of my earnings. I had a plan.

LONDON CALLING

Being a musician or working in the music business was a common dream of many teenagers at the time. I always wanted to be the performer and not the spectator, preferring to be part of the show instead of just watching. There was just one problem: I was shy and did not display any musical talent except for a brief dabble in playing trombone in elementary school. Since being a musician wasn't in the cards, I decided I wanted to be off stage, but still essential to the action. My plan was to save up my busboy earnings to start a record company.

It all started on Christmas 1979, when my dad gave me a copy of The Clash's *London Calling*. My musical tastes had been somewhat mainstream, with LPs from Foreigner ("Hot Blooded" being my favorite), Styx, and Toto occupying my turntable. However, The Clash cracked a door open into a new frontier: bands with lyrics that had a message. Their songs spoke to me like poetry:

> *I've been beat up I've been thrown*
> *Out but I'm not down, I'm not down*
> *I've been shown up, but I've grown up*
> *And I'm not down, I'm not down.*

On my own I faced a gang of jeering in strange streets
When my nerves were pumping and I
Fought my fear in, I did not run
I was not done
And I have lived that kind of day
When one of your sorrows will go away
It goes down and down and hit the floor
Down and down and down some more
Depression
But I know there'll be some way
When I can swing everything back my way
Like skyscrapers rising up
Floor by floor, I'm not giving up

– FROM "I'M NOT DOWN" BY THE CLASH

Even as a child, I enjoyed comeback stories where people over-came adversity and against all odds achieved what they sought. I was always rooting for the underdog. The greater the challenge, the more I liked the story. However, I could not fathom that one-day, I would be the fallen one trying to claw my way back. "I'm Not Down" was a comeback song that would later become my anthem.

I started buying alternative music fanzines, publications that were often Xeroxed and stapled together, then sold for a dollar in independent record stores. I skateboarded a few miles to get to Rhino Records on Westwood Boulevard to peruse the offer-ings. I learned of bands across Europe and the United States who were going DIY, or Do It Yourself. Forget trying to impress the major labels like Capitol Records, Atlantic and EMI. These bands were paying for their own recording time, getting the tapes mastered, and paying plants to press the records—all for a few thousand dollars. I was now 14 with a few thousand in the bank. *Hey—I realized—I could really do this!*

If anyone else could do it, I could do it too. Whatever I needed to learn, I would figure out. My busboy to record company plan was going to work! Now I just needed some bands to make a record with. I knew the bands I liked, but somehow I needed to connect with them.

I convinced my father to drop me off at the Whisky-A-Go-Go in Hollywood on Sunset Boulevard to go alone to the 8:00 PM all ages Saturday shows. I saw Britain's Killing Joke, local bands 45 Grave, Monitor, the Circle Jerks, Wasted Youth and others.

The youthful energy of the performers and the audience was contagious, and I slammed and stage dived with abandon. At school dances, I always felt awkward as I publicly displayed my lack of rhythm. However, at punk shows, I could freely join in the swirl of the mosh pit. No rhythm needed. I felt this was where I belonged.

"Do you need a ride?" I would be asked over and over from a parade of smiling men in nice cars as I stood at the bus stop across Sunset from the Whisky.

"No, thank you," I replied. "My dad is on his way to pick me up." I didn't understand why the locals in West Hollywood were so helpful. *"They all seem so friendly,"* I remember thinking. I didn't understand just how "friendly" they were trying to be until a couple years later.

YOUTH MANIFESTO

"Hi, my name is Jorge from Youth Manifesto," I said to Greg Ginn of Black Flag over the phone. "I want to interview Black Flag. When can we meet?" My strategy was to not ask if they wanted to be interviewed. Instead, I'd just ask when and where we could meet. It always seemed to work. Once I scheduled an interview, I would then scour through the band's lyrics and analyze them in order to craft relevant questions.

The more interviews I conducted, the more effective I was at extracting insight. I learned to only ask questions as needed to keep the conversation going and to allow the topics to wander. I didn't want to hear my voice on the tape; I wanted to hear theirs. I had discovered the art of listening.

I wasn't old enough to drive unaccompanied, so my mum or sisters would escort me to meet the bands. While they waited in the car or at a Winchell's donut shop, I interviewed Black Flag, Bad Religion, Saccharine Trust, Youth Brigade, RF7, and Louisiana's Red Rockers when they toured through L.A. My work was my play and my schooling. I was learning to research, ask, negotiate, reason, interpret, calculate, visualize, and create. However, there was an impediment to my education: school.

Although I was a Dean's List student through 9th grade, school had become mundane and unchallenging. By the second month of 11th grade, I passed the Graduate Equivalency Degree exam. However, I still had to get my parents' permission to leave school.

"Jorgie, are you sure this is what you want to do?" asked my dad. We were seated around the dining table in our living room. Even though I was now 15, my father still added the diminutive "-ie" to the end of my name. This was embarrassing in public, especially when he sometimes yelled "Jorgie" in a store or market. I'd return to him, but pretend I didn't know him.

"It's Jorge," I replied with emphasis on the "ge" ending, correcting my father and making sure he recognized my annoyance with the "-ie." He disregarded my correction. As he had graduated college, I expected him to be uncomfortable with my request. "I want to focus on my business," I chimed in hopefully.

"I left school when I was 14," my mother added, helpfully. I knew this, but appreciated her bringing it up at that moment. She grew up in England and went to a private boarding school on a scholarship, but needed to leave when her parents could no longer afford their share of the tuition. This was turbulent 1938, at the tail end of the Great Depression and the beginning of the Second World War. As the country plunged into blackouts and bombings, the government utilized a slogan to encourage the populace: "Keep Calm & Carry On." Her family income had shrunk and my mum had to take a job at a local library to contribute to the household.

"I can always go to college later if I change my mind," I said to soften the blow, even though I had no interest in the idea. Instead, I wanted to experience real-life challenges. My ancestors had faced trials before: my mother's parents had met in the First World War when my grandfather was called up into the army. As a soldier fighting in the trenches, he was gassed and shot in the eye by German soldiers. My grandmother was the military nurse who attended to him. Throughout his remaining years, my grandfather was haunted by his time in combat. My mother was often awakened as he sang war songs in his nightmares.

"He is a good boy. He works hard," my mother said. She had followed her dream to be an actress. At age 16, she was hired to work backstage at a theatre. Nine months later, she was chosen for a leading role as half-caste Tondelayo in *White Cargo*. At the time, half-caste was a common term in England to describe anyone mixed of Caucasian and conquered races. Today, half-caste is considered an offensive slur. Before performances, my mum was covered in brown makeup. This character was her breakthrough role, and she performed throughout England. Other roles such as Ophelia in *Hamlet* followed, and she eventually joined a touring company for many years. More than a decade later, as she performed on tour through the United States, she met my father in St. Louis.

"I am not getting into trouble. I want to explore," I said.

"Okay, Jorgie," said my dad.

I was out of school on my 16th birthday and free to chase my dreams, which filled my bountiful imagination. I would set my sights on a target, take the first step, then the second, and I thought I could do anything I set my mind to.

Once I eliminated the distraction of school, I used my busboy earnings to spend hours at Studio 9, a tiny and affordable recording studio in an almost-empty building at the corner of Hollywood Boulevard and Western Avenue in a seedy section of Hollywood. I would take the number 2 RTD bus along Sunset Boulevard, then skateboard the rest of the way to the studio. I thoroughly enjoyed the process of weaving through hours and hours of interviews, juxtaposing them with snippets of music, then editing everything into digestible and riveting tales. I entitled my creation *Youth Manifesto* and shared the almost-complete version with some of the participating bands. Jack Brewer from Saccharine Trust told me that Henry Rollins was impressed with my concoction. Soon, a representative from Greenworld Distribution called with an offer to exclusively distribute *Youth Manifesto* in the U.S. I was 16 when I negotiated the deal from my office on the corner of my family's kitchen table.

I then went back to the fanzines to go through the ads. I found one company to mass-produce the cassettes and another to print the covers, which were 8.5 × 11 hardbacks to which we affixed the tapes and then sealed into clear plastic bags. Within weeks, a semi-truck pulled up to my house to drop off thousands of cassettes. Shortly thereafter, another semi arrived with all the covers. I packaged these together at the kitchen table with the help of my mother and siblings, and soon, *Youth Manifesto* was being shipped nationwide.

Several positive reviews followed, including a short but complimentary mention in the *L.A. Weekly*. Shavedneck.com has the full tape posted online and observes that "the tape reflects well the almost utopian, if not naïve and idealistic values and morals espoused by the more intellectual of hardcores at the time." The liner notes read:

Between February and May of 1982, a number of American punk bands were asked for their ideas and views on America, religion, government, politics, war, hippies, and just about everything that affects our American society today. The main purpose in putting out YOUTH MANIFESTO is not that you agree with us, but just to make you aware of how we feel.

YOUTH MANIFESTO

BAD RELIGION   BLACK FLAG
SACCHARINE TRUST   R.F. 7
RED ROCKERS   YOUTH BRIGADE

SACCHARINE TRUST — Ed Colver

BLACK FLAG — Ed Colver

YOUTH BRIGADE — Glen Friedman

BAD RELIGION — Ed Colver

R.F.7 — Ed Colver

RED ROCKERS — Rick Rod

Between Febuary and May of 1982, a number of American punk bands were asked for their ideas and views on America, religion, government, politics, war, hippies, police, and just about everything that affects our American society today. The main purpose in putting out YOUTH MANIFESTO is not that you agree with us but just to make you aware of how we feel.

We offer thanks to all the bands and their recording and publishing companies AND Howie Klein (415), Daphna Edwards (Unicorn), Mike and Cynthia Franey, Gary Hirstuis, Anne Newbery, Bruce Gowers, Ron Gaudy, Ed Colver, Dream, Lisa Fancher (Fronties), Bo Clifford, Carrie at the Whisky, Joe at SST, Jordan at We Got Power, Steve at Rhino, Lester Edwards (ASR Recording), John Gillis (Studio 9), Better Youth Organization, all the Newberys, Brett, Neil Cooper (B.O.I.R.), Ben Jones (SEPAC), Mike Watt (New Alliance), Greg Ginn, Darron Hill, Felix Alanis (Smoke 7), Mark and Shawn Stern, Kathleen at ASR, Margaret Thompson, Esteban Caricedo, and everyone we forgot.

Produced by Jorge Newbery. Assistant Producers Rod Ellis and Charlene Gowers. Engineered by Rod Ellis. Cover Photo by Ed Colver. Cover Design by Anne Newbery. Edited and Mixed at Studio 9 in Hollywood. (An L.A. Rocks/Youth Manifesto production: (213) 394 - 6638. 1119 Colorado Avenue, Suite 107, Santa Monica CA 90601).

The first issue of YOUTH MANIFESTO has been copyrighted, 1982, by L.A. Rocks. The music excerpts have been used with permission and all rights belong to the respective recording and publishing companies. Broadcast, duplication, or reproduction of any part of YOUTH MANIFESTO is forbidden without written permission. All rights reserved.

There is always hope.

HAPPY TIMES

After my success, I started renting halls and promoting shows featuring my new band contacts, including Social Distortion, Circle One, Red Cross (later Redd Kross due to complaints by the Red Cross organization), and Youth Brigade. We needed a stage for one of the first shows, at the Happy Times Roller Rink at 83rd and Vermont in South Central Los Angeles. Mark Stern from Youth Brigade offered to build the stage if I would buy the materials.

The stage was huge and I had to store several 4-foot by 4-foot cubes in the street and driveway in front of my parents' house for a few days, much to the chagrin of some neighbors. On the day of the gig, I needed to rent a 24-foot stake truck in order to transport the stage to the roller rink. Although I had a driver's license by now, Sam's U Drive on Sepulveda would not rent to anyone under 18. Thus, my ever-supportive mum went with me and said she wanted to rent the truck. She did all the paperwork and drove the truck off the lot, which is where I took over the reins.

Social Distortion, Channel 3, Youth Brigade, Sin 34, Caustic Cause, and Bad Example performed in front of several hundred fans at Happy Times. But the event had many challenges. There was so many people in the rink that the air conditioning was unable to keep up and the place became stiflingly hot. Also, some of the stage cubes were covered with graffiti—although I found this kind of cool.

Some punks got into the DJ booth and started flinging vinyl disco records around the rink, inflicting lacerations on those unfortunate enough to be hit by airborne collections of Donna Summers and the Bee Gees. Worse, fans had to park on the streets in this rougher section of town and locals robbed and beat up a few of them as they walked to the rink. We let the ones who were mugged in for free.

It wasn't long before there was a platoon of police outside the rink. They let the show go on, but asked us to cancel the following week's show featuring England's Angelic Upstarts because they were concerned that more fans would be assaulted. I called the district commander the following week, offering more security and trying to find a means to have the show go on, but he counseled me that the risk was too great.

I listened to their advice and we cancelled the next Happy Times show. I was disappointed to back off, and dozens of fans still showed up only to find the roller rink closed. Surprise cancellations were something both fans and bands had grown accustomed to, as many local venues had started to ban punk bands due to punk-police clashes. We, of course, blamed the police.

THE SUNSET RIOTS

As word got out that I owned a stage, other promoters such as Goldenvoice started contacting me, looking to rent it. Just as Mr. Snodgrass of the *Herald Examiner* greeted me with initial amusement, many in the industry were equally tickled that I was 17 and in charge of the show, record company, stage, and magazine. However, I was reliable, on time, worked diligently, and pitched in whenever I could. Even if someone did not take me seriously at first, I demonstrated a work ethic that promptly offset any concerns about my age. I was getting paid to go to all these great shows, and every gig generated more and more graffiti, turning my stage into a mobile piece of art graced by punk legends.

I offered the stage for a few hundred dollars a show, undercutting the market. For each rental, I delivered and bolted the cubes together, then disassembled after the show. I rented the stage that was in place at SIR Studios on Jan. 8, 1983 for the T.S.O.L. (True Sounds of Liberty), Social Distortion, and Redd Kross concert when the Sunset Riots broke out. SIR Studios was just off Sunset Boulevard in Hollywood. There were about 2,500 lively fans packed inside. However, when I walked outside to get some tools from the truck, I beheld masses of police in riot gear who had surrounded SIR. I found this odd—*why were the riot police here when there was no riot?*

This was my first exposure to a "police riot," in which the police are responsible for instigating a conflict. At the time, such a concept was so completely alien to me, I figured that the police knew something I didn't.

If there were no police outside SIR that night, everyone would just have gone home after the show in a law-abiding manner, save for maybe minor graffiti or public urination violations by a few drunken fans. In general, massive police build-ups have provoked rioting throughout history, from the 1886 Haymarket Riots in Chicago following the police killing of four striking workers at McCormick Harvesting Company, to the 2014 Ferguson Riots in Missouri following the fatal shooting by police of unarmed African American teenager Michael Brown.

Upon hearing of the phalanx of riot police outside, Jack Grisham, the singer of T.S.O.L., urged everyone to sit down and let the police drag everyone out. Everyone listened and an anticipatory silence bristled through the crowd. However, after several minutes, nothing happened. People started getting up and leaving.

The peace broke once everyone went outside. Fueled by police warnings to disperse, some punks threw bottles. These acts of defiance should have been anticipated from a huge crowd of teens and young adults, and I am surprised that the police did not have more effective strategies of defusing these situations. Many of the officers looked like Catholic nuns ready to mete out some discipline. Gazes narrowed, skin paled and glistened with sweat, and muscles tensed and readied to pounce.

"Go ahead, throw one more bottle, you punks," the officers appeared to think as they eyed the kids outside SIR that night. *"Just give me an excuse to beat you dozens of times with this club. Let me work out some of this pent-up frustration."* This was well before hand-held video cameras and Rodney King, so as soon as a punk threw one projectile too many, the LAPD army had the justification they yearned for to indiscriminately dispense adrenaline-fueled drubbings on fans. This escalated into a full riot that shut down Sunset and several adjoining streets. Some fans split to avoid the pandemonium, while others were itching to rumble and joined the cops in escalating the situation. Although the raw tension was electric, I stayed calm.

I had been through this before at other shows and learned to walk away and avoid the chaos. I was appalled at the behavior of the police, but also by some of the punks. "Two wrongs don't make a right" is a well-worn cliché, but it was apt here. Setting fire to police cars to get back at the cops for beating your friend may have made a fan feel good for a moment, but in the end, this resulted in venues like SIR and the Whisky banning punk shows. We all lost.

Oddly, as I waited at a bus bench on some side street, my dad pulled up from out of nowhere in his trusty VW Squareback. He was just returning from a cocktail party and got caught in the traffic caused by the riot. By some random coincidence, he saw me and stopped.

"Jorgie," he said. I was 17 now, but the diminutive "-ie" persisted. "What happened?"

"It's Jorge," I said, correcting my father. I spoke loudly to be heard over the din of wailing sirens and buzzing helicopters. "The police started beating people up after the show and it turned into a riot," I replied, unhesitatingly. I knew that he would understand.

Just then, two fans turned the corner and walked towards us. The young man, about my age and a skinhead, had his shirt off and was stumbling. The girl, a little younger with a red Mohawk and studded leather jacket with a large "Exploited" patch on the front, was walking with her arm wrapped tightly around him to keep him upright. She held a T-shirt against his face. The shirt was saturated with blood.

"Do you need some help?" my father and I asked, almost in unison.

"We'll be okay," said the girl. "Our car is right up here. Thanks."

"The police are horrible," my father said. My dad had been beaten and jailed by police for protesting in Argentina when he was a college student. He was not a fan of them, and I think he was pleased to see that I was carrying on his "question authority" beliefs. I could see in his face, though, that he was also dismayed that police brutality continued unabated and was shaken by the bloodied skinhead. *"That could have been me 40 years ago,"* I imagined him thinking.

"It was calm until the police showed up," I said. "I need to wait for everything to clear to get the stage back home."

"Okay," my dad said. "I will see you in the morning." Eventually, everyone had either gone home or to jail and I was able to get back in to retrieve the stage. On these stage rental nights, I often returned home in the wee hours of the morning, but my parents never minded. Neither of them ever tried to dissuade me from exploring in life, wherever my wandering mind led me, even if I was a teenager sitting alone at 1:00 AM on a bus bench in Hollywood just blocks away from a massive riot.

STRAIGHT EDGE

My punk friends felt like society's outcasts. They were from all over Southern California, came from many different schools, and were mostly in their teens and early 20s. All my life, I had been a loner and felt like I did not fit in; however, now I sensed that I somehow belonged. Although my punk friends were mostly white, middle class, and "privileged," they were often tormented. Some were ignored by their parents, gay, abused, or, like me, just didn't fit into society's mold. We had trouble doing what was expected of us and yearned to find a better way, to build a better world for us and everybody else. For some, alcohol and drugs filled a void and helped dull whatever pained them. For others, the substances helped them feel like they fit in.

Me and a few others saw what excessive alcohol and drugs were doing to our friends and opted not to partake. This became the straight edge movement, popularized by Washington D.C.'s Minor Threat, which featured a clear-headed lifestyle punctuated by no alcohol, no drugs, and no indiscriminate sex. Suddenly, nerds like me were cool. The punk scene afforded me the first group of solid friends I ever had: Kimberly, an African American girl who I had a crush on; Natalie Boot, a talented artist; and Jordan Schwartz and Dave Markey, who published *We Got Power* fanzine. No Jordache jeans or Members Only jackets were required. With punk, everyone was welcome—even me—and especially those whom society had kicked down.

SLEEPING BAGS TOPPED BY MOHAWKS AND SPIKED HAIR
Some of my shows featured bands from out of town and my parents often let them spend the night in our home, so they could save money on motels. My family would wake up to a living room full of sleeping bags topped by Mohawks and spiked hair belonging to punk luminaries such as Ribzy, White Cross and Whipping Boy, an all-African American group from San Francisco.

"Where is the best place to get breakfast?" I remember the members of Whipping Boy ask, as they awoke groggily the morning after a gig.

"I can cook you scrambled eggs," my ever-hospitable mother offered.

My mum would then distribute platefuls of eggs and bacon to the band members, who proceeded to chow down at the dining table on our terrace.

"Thanks for the place to crash and the breakfast. The food was great," Whipping Boy's lead singer said, as they prepared to drive on to the next city on their tour.

"They all look so tough, but they are so nice," my mum observed after they left. Our unofficial punk hotel taught me that people generally treat you the way you treat them.

SPIC

My family was always welcoming, especially to those who appeared disenfranchised. However, some of our neighbors had different beliefs as to who belonged in our neighborhood. When my parents bought the house in 1965, some neighbors took to maliciously calling us "the gypsies."

We preferred to think of ourselves as eclectic. My dad was an architect for IBM and my mum was a British actress, who had sidelined her career to marry and raise five children: my sisters, Charlene and Anne, and my brothers, Alastair and Charles. Our family style was more wild oat than white bread, with our hair often long and clothes more hippie than Buster Brown. My father practiced Tai Chi, and my parents employed a loose and lenient style of parenting probably reflective of, well, gypsies.

Although neighbors bandied about the word in a derogatory manner, I don't think my parents considered the term negative

My mum and I in the backyard of the unofficial punk hotel

and they never seemed to care what our neighbors said or did. If they were confronted with insults, they appeared to let them slide off their backs. They were great examples to me, as I would also face some mindless hatred.

"Hey spic," kids would taunt me at elementary school and in my neighborhood. I understood "spic" to be more or less equivalent of "nigger" for Hispanics. My father was Hispanic, my mother was white, and our neighborhood was almost all white. Brentwood Elementary, my school, was much the same.

"Fight, fight, a nigger and a white" were the first words of a common schoolyard rhyme sung out loud by many kids, most of whom I doubt were trying to be racist. It was far worse that adults and teachers would hear the rhyme and do nothing to stop it.

Following my parents' example, I typically let the jeers slide off my back. I heard them, but ignored them. I think my lack of a reaction helped defuse the verbal attackers. When I was maybe eight or nine, the neighborhood's first African American family, the Elliots, moved in. Mark Elliot, who was about the same age as me, likely got tormented worse than me. I became friends with him, prompted in part by my realization that he was having trouble fitting in, a feeling I shared.

Mrs. Elliot once offered my mum a ride as she walked the steep hill up Acari Drive. As my mother relayed the story, Mrs. Elliot made the offer, then added "if that's okay," fearing that she, as an African American, had offended my white mum by offering her a ride. My mum had toured the Southern U.S. as part of a play troupe in the 1950s and had shared with me her shock at the treatment of African Americans, who were forced to use separate theater entrances, water fountains and even sections of public buses. Once, she boarded a bus and, seeing no other seats available, sat in the African American section at the back. Some whites exhorted her to move, but she was aghast at the degrading segregation and remained seated in defiance. At that time, African Americans such as Rosa Parks were arrested for sitting in seats intended for whites, but apparently there were no laws to arrest my white mother for sitting in the African American section. My mum accepted Mrs. Elliot's offer of a ride.

Further, my mum went out of her way to be neighborly to Mrs. Elliot, realizing that they were likely getting the same cool reception as we had as the "gypsies." One particularly inhospitable couple lived next door to us. My father would playfully call them "monsters" when I was just a few years old. I was too young to pronounce the full word "monsters," so I called them the "moes," which is how the whole family referred to them for the rest of our lives.

Although my parents and family generally welcomed our musician guests, the neighbors were not thrilled, and at some point, even drafted a petition complaining of noise as some bands did tune up a bit in the garage. They also complained about the graffiti-covered stage which was periodically stored in the street; the rented stake truck that often rumbled home in the early morning; the sinister-looking band vans parked in front of our house; and other purported inconveniences. A police officer lived across the street and had always been friendly to me.

One day, as John Macias and the other mostly Hispanic band members of Circle One drove off, he called me over.

"Your friends like that," he said, motioning to the departing van. "Those are the same guys I arrest every day. You need to choose your friends more carefully." He and I never spoke again.

Although my family never complained, in retrospect, I realize that I pushed the limits of being a good neighbor and imposed on my family with the frequent guests. We once had an independent record company producer from San Francisco named Michael stay at our home for two weeks straight. He was probably in his late 20s, tall and lanky with a Mohawk. We met when I sold my records to a store he managed. He was learning the L.A. punk scene and we went to several shows together. He was a nice guy, but he smoked incessantly. He partook outdoors, but wherever he walked there was a haze that followed him—like Pigpen in Charlie Brown. My mum and Anne took to referring to him as "Smelly Mike." They were not trying to be mean, but he really did reek.

I have many pleasant memories of my punk era. I remember a day when my family was having a garage sale and a beat up van pulled up and all the members of Social Distortion emerged. They were there to meet with me, but they perused the garage sale offerings for a while, even buying something. Recollecting this story will always generate a good laugh from my mum.

VANDALISM
I vividly recall one night at Whittier's T-Bird Roller Rink, which

had rented the stage for a show featuring The Vandals. After setting up the stage, the promoter asked me to go pick up the band as their van had broken down. Thus, I drove the stake truck to pick them and their equipment up from their rehearsal space in Long Beach. Luckily, they were headlining, so we made it back in time. The show went great and, sometime after midnight, I disassembled the stage. The Vandals and I then loaded the stage cubes and their equipment onto the truck to return them to Long Beach. Around 2:00 AM, we were driving in the fast lane of a fog-engulfed 710 freeway when we heard a thud followed by a crash.

"The Gypsies" according to our neighbors. I'm the baby.

"What was that?" said one of The Vandals, suddenly alert after dozing off.

"I think it was one of the cubes," I said nervously, as the rear view mirror dimly reflected a cube splintering in the fast lane. "Should we go back?"

"No way, we're liable to get killed walking on the freeway with all this fog," said the previously dozing Vandal. "Keep rolling."

"But someone's going to have an unpleasant wake-up call," said another Vandal. "They'll be driving in the fog and..."

"Wham-Bam," said the previously dozing Vandal. "They collide with the punk rock stage."

"How'd that happen?" I asked. I always tied the stage cubes down tight to avoid a situation like this. "Did you all tie everything down?"

"Yeah, yeah," said the previously dozing Vandal. "We tied everything down tight."

I had my doubts. This was the first time I ever had anyone help me load the stage. The only likely explanation was that one of them did not tie down the orphaned cube.

"Whoever hits it could get hurt," I said, anxious but getting more annoyed realizing that one of The Vandals was the likely culprit. "And have major damage to their car."

"Don't worry," said the Vandal. "If someone hits it, the damage will be more like Vandalism."

They all laughed. I chuckled a bit, but still felt bad, hoping that no one would get hurt if the cube suddenly appeared out of the fog in the fast lane.

This was just one of maybe two dozen cubes, so future shows had a small section of the stage missing. The stage was still fully functional and safe—plus the missing piece was somewhat apropos considering the eccentric acts that graced the stage.

DEAD BEFORE 30

In 1983, I released "Are You Afraid?" by local hardcores Circle One on Upstart Records, my fledgling record label. Albums by Red Scare, Stalag 13, Killroy, and Shattered Faith soon followed, along with a shorter EP by Hated Principles. Most of the records sold several thousand copies. I even started Upstart Distribution to help distribute records by other DIY'ers nationwide. Several of the albums received rave reviews and, during the punk revival of the early 1990s, other labels re-released some of Upstart's releases as CDs. My busboy to record mogul fantasy had become reality at age 17. However, in later years, I would find out just how harsh reality can be: 40 percent of the singers on my record label's LPs died before age 30.

Tragically, Bobbi Brat, the lead singer of Red Scare, was felled by stomach cancer. In 1987, Music Connection named her Top Club Draw in Southern California. However, as her career blossomed, so did the cancer. Bobbi appeared aware of her looming demise as she wrote one of her last songs:

> *Save me a seat on that salvation train*
> *Open up the gates, I'm comin in from the rain*
> *No more sorrow, no more pain*
> *Save me a seat on that salvation train*
> *I close my eyes and I hear the angels sing*
> *I close my eyes and see the light of their heavenly wings*
> — FROM "SALVATION TRAIN" BY BOBBI BRAT

Bobbi died in 1988. She was only 26.

In 1991, John Macias, the lead singer of Circle One, was shot dead by a Santa Monica police officer. He was 29. According to officers, John was "yelling something about God" as he assaulted two citizens. When police arrived, instead of diffusing the situation, one officer shot him. The police reported that John "had a jacket wrapped around his hand," which I suppose implied that he could have been armed. However, like Michael Brown in Ferguson over two decades later, John didn't have a weapon on him. Paradoxically, again like Michael Brown, the police reported that Macias continued to advance on the officers after being shot. As a result, the police felt justified in continuing to shoot at Macias, who died with four shots to the chest and neck.

Circle One drummer Jody Hill shared stunning recollections about John in 2013 on *There's Something Hard In There*, an online blog that is reminiscent of the fanzines of the early 1980s:

What stands out the most about John today is a lot of people, in books, in documentaries, and many other forms of media, talk about him and they are talking about someone who was not the John I knew. Was he a bad ass? Yes, he could be. Would he stand up against cops, bullies, concert promoters? Yes. Was he violent at times? Yes, again. Did he get shot and killed by the cops three days after our last performance with him? Sadly, yes. He didn't get shot and killed because of all the things I just mentioned.

John really cared about people and the scene he was involved in. He believed in God, but a lot of his actions in that area were caused by his mental illness. We were not a Christian punk band. John sang about what was going on in his head. Later on, we found out there was a lot going on in his head that he didn't have control over, and by the time we knew he had problems, he was dead. Like I said at the beginning, I have read that John was black, a gang leader, a born again, etc., but all these statements are always written by people who don't know him. He still makes an impact in my life 22 years later. The new band I am in with Mike Vallejo (Manwray) has two songs that in some ways are about John. He is the first person I think about when we play them. So when you talk to people, remember, a lot of people you talk to only knew him for a short time and some, if not most, really didn't know him at all.

I remember one day in 1983 driving with John to pick up his mother from her job in Culver City. I could tell by their inter-action that John was loved and very loving in return. He was a leader, smart, and impassioned. However, despite family, friends, and fans, he seemed to have trouble fitting in and finding where he belonged in America. I shared the feeling.

Although some of the records generated good earnings, I spent a lot on great studios, the best record mastering, and quality covers. At the time, some DIY'ers were putting out LPs recorded on 4-track recorders at home or even cassette players. I wanted to deliver a high quality product and did not pay as much attention as I should have to whether delivering a good product sacrificed profits. Further, I extended credit to many stores across the country and not everyone paid on time and some did not pay at all. I would diligently follow up, but they were often hundreds or thousands of miles away, so I was unable to apply too much pressure—plus, my disposition was too nice to be threatening.

This created challenges in my cash flow and the distribution company had trouble paying other labels. This was my first taste of credit and the challenges that could arise from it. In the end, the money I earned went back into the company as the excitement of doing the deals often outweighed the potential profits. Most importantly though, I proved that I could do what I set my mind to and learned real-life lessons that I would never have been exposed to in my final two years of high school or college.

John Macias (1962–1991) Photo: Alison Braun

CHAPTER TWO

Olympic Dreams to Loan Originator

"In cycling, 'Fred' is code for newbie—someone whose knowledge is incomplete. Naturally, it's the last thing anyone wants to be called."

— PATRICK BRADY, *HOW TO LOOK LIKE A CYCLIST*

IN LATE 1984, I WAS 19. MY TRADITIONAL SCHOOLING WAS well behind me, and my mind was seeking a new pursuit. I had accomplished my record company goal, and the fun had since diminished. A trend had emerged in the 12 years since I'd landed myself a paper route: I needed to prove I could excel at something and, once I did, I lost interest and needed a new challenge.

That year, the Olympics were in Los Angeles and American Alexi Grewal won the cycling road race. Coincidentally, my dad bought me a used 10-speed bike for my 19th birthday. With the Olympics as inspiration, I now had a new goal: bike racer.

NEVER, EVER LOOK BACK

I bought a bunch of bike racing books and read that the top riders were riding 500 miles a week. Within a few months, I was riding 500 miles a week, which is hours and hours on a bike, especially since my pace was much slower than elite cyclists. I joined some group training rides, although I always felt like I did not fit in. Then I read an article in *City Sports* magazine that said Olympian John Howard was training cyclists. I called him up and asked him to coach me. Howard agreed and brought me in for a lesson. And despite the fact that I rode hundreds of miles a week, he started me at the very beginning.

"What are you wearing under your shorts?" he asked shortly after we began our first training ride. He apparently noticed the ripple of underwear under my Lycra cycling shorts.

"Briefs," I said.

"You shouldn't wear anything," he said, sounding a bit astonished at my naiveté.

"Really?" I asked.

"Yes," he said. "There's a gas station up here on the right. Stop there and get those off." I proceeded to the gas station restroom and removed the briefs. I suppose, "don't wear underwear" is such basic cycling knowledge that the books didn't mention it. In bike racer parlance, I was a Fred. As I pedaled through my 500 miles a week, I had wondered how top cyclists dealt with such crotch discomfort. No underwear was the simple answer, but it was one that never occurred to me. Removing my underwear brought me one step away from being a Fred and one step closer to being a bike racer.

When I first started racing in the fall of 1985, I had no idea of the unspoken rules of the pack, such as keeping a straight line when I rode and mitigating sudden stops. Further, although my equipment and clothing were functional, I did not have the cool European brand names such as Campagnolo. Bike racers also shave their legs to improve aerodynamics and lessen road rash in crashes. However, I could not bring myself to shave my legs. I remembered that parade of men offering me rides on Sunset Boulevard as I waited for my dad after the Whisky gigs. I was already self-conscious in skintight Lycra with no underwear. What would happen if I had no hair on my legs? While my looks still may not have fit in, I was relentless in my training and did everything the books said I should do. And it was paying off. Though I had been bringing up the rear on group rides just months before, I started to show some promise.

I started working at Bikeology, a local bike shop, as a part time stock clerk. The job provided me discounts when buying equipment and clothing. Additionally, the schedule was flexible to allow me time to train. I would ask other riders about local training rides and soon started showing up at rides that included top riders and even Olympians. I thought it was okay for me to join in, yet I struggled to keep up and often ended up finishing alone far behind.

Undeterred, I kept following the books and even invested in a heart rate monitor long before they were commonplace. I read that Jacques Buyer, who in 1981 became the first American to race in the Tour de France, was utilizing a heart rate monitor and Anaerobic Threshold Training up long climbs. Not stocked in stores, I ordered the monitor by mail.

I would strap this box half the size of a paperback book to my wrist and the cable would run up my arm to a band that went around my chest. It was cumbersome and awkward, especially relative to the sleek monitors of today.

I learned how training within certain ranges maximized my body's ability to sustain difficult efforts for extended periods. The goal was to ride at a level just a fraction below my maximum. If I pushed just a bit over my limit, I would go into oxygen debt and my body would soon force me to stop. And stopping wasn't an option.

I was a "Fred" in 1985

BREAKTHROUGH

A breakthrough came on a training ride in January 1986 in the San Fernando Valley with Olympian Thurlow Rogers and other top local riders. I had ridden with this group before and finished well behind. However, on this day, I was keeping up and felt strong. Everyone else was talking, but I was silent, focused and trying to stay relaxed and calm. I now looked the same as everyone else, having finally shaved my legs to try to fit in. Still, I knew I was different. I was a loner. I felt uncomfortable in the group and, when we were at the base of a very long climb, I wanted to escape. I surged ahead. Since I was a Fred, I was ignored. However, soon enough, I was out of sight and pedaling furiously. John Howard had taught me to never, ever look back, as this is a sign of weakness. Throughout my cycling career, and all my life, I have always remembered this.

I always imagine my chasers are just a few feet behind, ready to pounce the moment I let up. This time I focused forward and tried to stay loose as I willed myself up this never-ending climb. I was in my first cycling burn zone and kept thinking that I was going to hear the breaths of the chasers anytime as they blew past me. However, as the summit came into view, no breaths could be heard. I was absolutely spent by the time I reached the top, still out front. The next guy to finish seemed a bit astonished and said something like "good ride," but I was hardly acknowledged by the others. On the outside, I was quiet, focused and determined, but inside I was thinking *"Fred, loner, outcast, spic, whatever—I beat you all today!"*

LEARNING FROM FAILURE

For bike racing amateurs, Category 4 is beginner and Category 1 is elite, and at the time, there were less than 300 Category 1's in the United States. By virtue of participating in a handful of Category 4 races in late 1985, I began moving up the chain. At the start of 1986, I was racing as a Category 3 racer; but when I won the Category 3 division of the Borrego Springs Stage Race in February (after a performance that was better than many of the Category 2s), District Rep. Steve Ball upgraded me to Category 2 for my next race: the Lancaster Road Race. With a few miles to go, there was a breakaway of about 10 riders out front and I was in the next group. Nervous that I would fare poorly in a sprint at the end, I pedaled ahead of the chase pack with a few miles left. Any known rider would have been run down immediately.

I was still an unknown to most and a Fred to others, so they let me go. I was in a burn zone, trying to stay calm and focusing on keeping my cadence high, back flat, and upper body relaxed. Although they came close to catching me at the end, they didn't and I took 11th place, enough for a small share of the prize money that was paid to the top 15. More than that, this performance was a validation that I was now a bike racer who could compete at a high level. However, the rest of the year was full of uneven performances as I tried to learn the subtleties of racing. Nevertheless, District Rep. Ball appeared to take note of my promise and upgraded me to the elite Category 1.

Southern California's moderate weather enables a long bike-racing season, and I was able to race almost every weekend from February to November, plus some weekdays. Races are

On my way to a 2nd place finish at 1986 Yuma-Blythe-Yuma race. This was one of the early "ultra" bike races and close to 200 miles.

unpredictable and the most successful racers only win occasionally. Thus, all racers lose a lot of races. It could be frustrating, of course, but I used my frequent losses as opportunities to reflect and improve as an athlete and as a person. As is common in life, I learned a lot more from my losses than my successes, but I enjoyed my time on the podium far more than my time in the middle of the pack.

In June 1987, at the Southern California State Championships, I finished 2nd overall and followed this up with a 44th place finish at the National Championships in Boulder, Colo., a few weeks later. I'd hoped these performances would help me gain a foothold in the top ranks of my team, sponsored by ICN Pharmaceuticals. However, in the fall, I was not chosen to join my team at the Vulcan Tour, a major stage race in Redding, Calif.

Although my high placings were proof of my abilities, I was still a newcomer to the top ranks and was often passed over in favor of longer-established riders—even though their recent performances did not measure up to mine. Nevertheless, an unexpected phone call would provide me the opportunity to prove myself.

VULCAN TOUR

Just days before the Vulcan Tour was to begin, ICN team captain Thurlow Rogers called to let me know that another team, KHS Suntour, needed a rider. I joined the rival team and rode strongly through the first few stages—better than most of my ICN teammates who had been selected over me. On our longest day, a road race of over 150 miles, I noted that Sprint points would be awarded to the first three riders to finish each of the first eight of 15 laps. The Sprints competition was a race within a race that rewarded the leader with a green jersey, just like in the Tour de France. The intention of the competition is to keep the early race lively and entertaining. Because this was the longest stage, other riders would likely be trying to conserve their energy. Each lap consisted of 10 very hilly miles—it wouldn't be easy—but I knew that day represented the best opportunity to win the Sprints competition against a field of Olympians and National Champions.

On that morning, I decided I would try to escape the pack early on and embark on a "suicide mission," in which I would ride as hard as I could for as long as I could in order to garner as many points as possible. This "suicide" strategy gets its name from the anticipation that an early breakaway will likely be caught and the rider(s) swallowed by the pack and spat out the back, left to drop out or complete the race on their own well behind the other riders. However, suicide missions occasionally result in wins.

A few miles in, we came to the first long climb. I accelerated up the right side of the pack, moving full steam ahead with my plan. But as the sun beat down on me, I started to doubt the wisdom of my strategy. I realized how hot it was, how many miles and stages lay ahead, and wondered whether I was simply setting myself up to bonk. I thought maybe I should just stay in the safety of the pack, where others shared the effort of cutting through the wind.

"Watch it asshole! Fucking Fred," screamed a Reebok rider, who I had errantly nudged. My insecurities jolted through me, and my response was to escape. I rode off the front of the pack with another Reebok rider on my wheel. As we gained ground, the other rider said, "We should be able to stay away a long time." We took turns breaking the wind and were soon out of the pack's sight and, presumably, out of mind. The Reebok rider won the first sprint and took the points, but I still earned points as the second to cross the line.

On the next long climb, the Reebok rider had mechanical difficulties—his chain was making loud grinding noises. He fell back and I kept going. *"Maybe this was a little Karmic payback for his teammate's petulance?"* I wondered. I was now sole leader by several minutes on a pack filled with America's cycling stars! I was pedaling intently, trying to keep focused, relaxed, and calm as the TV truck pulled up alongside to get better shots of this unknown loner.

I remember going up the climb when the KHS Suntour van was going down in the opposite direction—the team manager's eyes practically popped out of his head when he saw me. One sprint win, another lap, two sprint wins, another lap, another sprint win, and on I went. I was in a burn zone and excited, but I needed to remain calm and focused. Most importantly, I never looked back. I knew my competition was somewhere behind me, ready to pounce.

I knew my suicide mission meant I would likely be overtaken at some point—that was all too often the name of the game—but I kept willing myself to cross the sprint line one more time. After just another lap, I was green jersey leader "on the road," meaning that if the race stopped right then, I would be awarded the jersey that I craved. This was my breakthrough role, like when my mum was cast as Tondelayo. The jersey would be a wearable emblem of my triumph. I kept going, winning all the sprints because I was so far ahead. My burn zone intensified as my body started to tire and as the pack started to close in.

Eventually, a chase group including Rogers, another ICN teammate and National Champion Doug Smith, and Olympic Gold Medalist Alexi Grewal caught up with me. I was now racing wheel-to-wheel with the guy who first inspired me to get into cycling and whose riding style I had tried to emulate. I was in awe, but felt I was where I belonged.

They caught me less than a mile from the next sprint. There

were probably still another 70 to 80 miles to go and I was absolutely spent. Knowing this was my last chance for points, I attacked one more time and, as I neared the sprint line, I was caught and passed by just one rider, receiving 2nd place points for the lap.

At the base of the next climb, Alexi Grewal pulled alongside me, "Good work." His words were spoken with respect; they were words to a peer, rather than a Fred. It felt good, but I knew as I heard his words that my race day at the front was over. Now, I had to pay the suicide piper as I fell behind and struggled to continue after my early exertion. I had to finish in order to stay in the race and claim the green jersey for the next stage. I kept riding, albeit slower, and eventually finished well behind the leaders. I was exhausted, but the green jersey was mine.

After eating, showering, and taking a nap, I ended up at a Subway sandwich shop and bumped into Rogers and Smith. Both congratulated me, with Smith being ever the gentleman, marveling at how I attacked as soon as I was caught. Smith would later be chosen to be on the cover of a Wheaties box, a well-deserved honor. I proudly wore that green jersey on many rides after that.

OLYMPIC DREAMS

The following season was 1988, an Olympic year that harbored much promise. I was 22, still working part time at Bikecology, and was now sponsored by the KHS Suntour team, which covered some of my equipment, entry fees, travel, and other expenses. Through the spring, I rode strongly, but did not generate the big results I had hoped for. In retrospect, this was just my third season of serious racing and my results were bound to plateau as I still had a lot to learn. However, I was too impatient. I wanted to move to the next level.

I earned a berth at the Olympic Trials, held in Spokane, Wash. I finished in 42nd place. It was good, but I was intent on much more. I crashed badly and stupidly in one of the Trials' events, taking a tight corner much too fast and ending up sprawled amongst the crowd on the sidewalk. My body was unhurt, but my hopes were shattered. Needless to say, I did not make the Olympic Team.

SPENCO 500

Unsatisfied, I set my sights on the Spenco 500, a 500-mile non-stop bike race in Waco, Texas in October 1988. The event was televised on ESPN. My preparation included Thursday long rides alone up the Pacific Coast Highway and into the Santa Monica Mountains, which extended to 140 miles, all rode at a heart rate of 130 or greater. At this point, I measured my resting heart rate every morning; it was often in the low 30 beats per minute range and sometimes as low as 28 or 29 beats per minute, which was on par with the top athletes in the world.

My father and brother Charles were my crew for the Spenco 500, handing me a water bottle full of UltraEnergy, a calorically dense concoction that tasted like chocolate milk, as I completed each 25-mile lap. I lined up with the solo riders, including prior year winner Steve Speaks of Schwinn. We started before the relay riders, which included eventual Tour

After winning the prologue at Redlands Bicycle Classic, 1988. That night, a timing error was discovered and I dropped to 73rd place.

de France champion Lance Armstrong, who was a teenager at the time. I do not recall any interaction with Armstrong, as he was still relatively unknown, although I had started hearing about performance-enhancing drugs and blood doping around this time. Maintaining the straightedge lifestyle I adopted as a punk, I did not partake and was confident that a healthy diet and disciplined training were the ingredients to cycling success.

For the solo riders in the Spenco 500, the burn zone came when the relay riders caught up to us and sped by. We were allowed to draft and ride in their wind-breaking wake, which we all tried to do. However, we had already been on the road for six or more hours and the relay riders had fresh legs. I barely hung on to the lead group of solo riders, which included Speaks and a handful of others. In the end, we covered over 500 miles in around 21 hours. With a weak finishing sprint, I ended up 4th overall.

TOUR OF MEXICO
Next, I looked to the Tour of Mexico in November 1988 as a new opportunity to vault to a higher level. This was a 21-day stage race, which featured several Mexican teams as well as national teams from around the world. I did not get chosen for the U.S. team.

Undeterred, I flew to Mexico City with *Winning Magazine* reporter Bill Blake. Bill spoke Spanish and we were at the sign-in area of the host hotel asking every team if they needed a rider. "Need a rider?" we asked. I didn't speak Spanish, but Bill taught me the short phrase. Finding a team was a long shot and I was truly pushing the envelope to put myself where I wanted to be.

With less than half an hour to go, all the teams had signed in and I was contemplating my return to the U.S., when the news hit: "A Costa Rican rider was hit by a car." Although the rider survived, he was too injured to race. Thus, this tragic news put me on the Costa Rican National Team.

The next day, all the riders rode our bikes parade-style through the streets of Mexico City with spectators five deep on every street. The procession ended in front of the "Palacio Nacional," a stately complex that has been the palace for the ruling class of Mexico since the Aztec empire. Here, the racing began with a pistol shot by the President of Mexico. On the road, I was now a "tico," which is a friendly nickname for Costa Ricans.

I flatted on the first stage and, after receiving a replacement wheel, was trying to catch up to the field using the caravan of support vehicles for some wind cover, a common tactic. The other countries' vehicles were cooperative, except for my home country. The U.S. vehicle sped up and moved to the left of the road in order to eliminate any benefit to me as I passed them. I caught the pack eventually and the stage finished with all the riders together, so I survived day one.

In the subsequent days, my placing gradually rose higher than any other tico or American. I gained the most time on a stage that featured a burn zone of high crosswinds, which decimated the pack. I stayed in the lead group of maybe 30, as we rotated in an efficient echelon. By the end of the day, the 30 of us gained several minutes on everyone else. I was in 21st overall and *El Diario*, a Spanish-language daily in Los Angeles, was now publishing daily updates on my efforts. My family and friends in Southern California were now able to follow my quest in each day's paper. The hilliest stages were at the end and, being a strong climber, I expected these would provide an opportunity for me to increase my position further.

With less than a week to go, I was at lunch in Guadalajara, the end point of the day's stage. We must have arrived late to the lunch because it was being cleaned up almost as soon as it was served. A slow eater, I didn't get to consume much and left starving. We had a bus ride to the next day's starting city. As I settled in on the bus, I saw that others had brought PowerBars and other snacks for the ride. All I had was water.

Then I discovered that the bus ride was three hours long. I had to eat constantly on and off the bike in order to replace all the calories I was burning as we raced several hours each day. I was always diligent about promptly refueling; however, I slipped up that day. My stomach was gnawing for the full duration of what felt like the longest bus ride of my life.

When we finally arrived later that night, eating was my first priority. I ate a lot, finally satiating my empty stomach, and turned in for the night. It wasn't long before I shot awake with a sharp pain in my belly; something I consumed disagreed with me. Soon, I was huddled over the toilet, throwing up everything I had eaten for dinner and making a mess around the commode.

The next day, as I rolled to the starting line, I received some media attention. And though I certainly didn't feel my best after the intestinal gymnastics of the night before, I answered all their questions optimistically. I was 21st and well in contention at the start, but by the end of the stage, I had lost over an hour and had fallen to around 95th place. I was out of contention.

Climbing with the leaders in the 1988 Tour of Mexico, intent on a breakout race. Instead, my face ended up planted over a commode.

My teammates tried to cheer me up, but I knew I had lost a great opportunity. I started that next day, but was still weak and only lasted about 10 miles before I was behind and pulled off to the side of the road. I waited for Costa Rica's team van and climbed in, giving up on my Tour de Mexico 1988. I was in total despair and searched for a lesson in my defeat.

BLAMING MYSELF

In retrospect, my performances in late 1988 at the Spenco 500 and the Tour of Mexico represented the apex of my cycling career. I was in the best shape of my life and I could compete internationally. I was just 23 and needed to be patient, to learn more, and take some comfort in my progress. Many racers compete at the highest levels into their 30s. I should have been looking forward to all that I could accomplish.

Instead, I was discouraged. I blamed myself for my Tour of Mexico defeat. I decided that I needed to train more and lose some weight. Lower levels of body fat and weight will generally improve performance. However, I was already ultra-lean with 165 pounds on a 6′ 2″ frame, sporting massive leg muscles. I didn't have weight to lose.

I wanted my Tour of Mexico loss to teach me something that would propel me to greatness. However, in hindsight, I had done almost everything as best I could. I did err in not eating enough early on the day into Guadalajara, not packing food for the long bus ride, and unknowingly eating something bad that evening. These were minor missteps, easily correctable for future races.

I should have been content with a performance that was on track to deliver a top 20 or maybe even top 10 international stage race performance on my first try. I should have rejoiced in all the good I had accomplished and realized that new opportunities would arrive soon. I should have rested a bit and then resumed my balanced and focused training, which had propelled me so far already.

Instead, I turned on myself. In addition to trying to take pounds off a body with little fat to spare, I eliminated the two easy riding days from my weekly schedule, changing them to intense days as well. I started eating tons of cabbage and lettuce, which filled up my stomach and gave me the sensation of being full without delivering a sufficient number of calories to support my training output. As a result, I lost weight, getting down to the lower 150s. My mum and sister Anne took to calling me

"Skull" as I was so gaunt. They teased me in a joking fashion, although I think my mum was truly concerned about how thin I had become.

CATHY

By February, I placed highly in one of the races near Fresno, Calif., which many national team hopefuls participate in. However, I soon developed bronchitis. I could still train and compete at a reasonably high level, but hacked and coughed a lot. It wasn't pleasant, but I was functional. My condition went on like that for months because I never took the time to heal my body. I should have rested and rebuilt, but instead my mind started wandering, seeking a new pursuit.

"What do you do again?" I asked Cathy Hertz, the girlfriend of my VitaCrunch teammate Jack VanDerVeen. Cathy always had a nice car and appeared to be financially comfortable.

"I help arrange mortgages for families buying homes, making improvements, consolidating bills," she answered.

"How much do you make?" I inquired.

"Around $3,000 monthly," Cathy replied. To me, this sounded like she was winning the lottery every month. I was earning $1,000 a month, a combination of part time earnings at Bikeology and race winnings split with teammates. This was financially viable only because I lived at home with my parents. I was 24 with no college degree and just a GED.

"How can I get a job in mortgages?" I asked, feeling a bit embarrassed. She had no reason to believe that I would be good in business, but I knew I was smart and could out-work anyone. I recognized that there could only be a modest number of elite cyclists in the world, and an even smaller number who actually make a good living from it. However, there are legions of successful businessmen in the world. If I could apply my extraordinary determination, focus, and work ethic to mortgages, then I could succeed.

"Well, first you need a real estate license," Cathy said. I soon started taking the required correspondence courses and then, mentored by Cathy, I took the real estate salesperson's exam. In January 1990, I received the results: I had passed! I called Cathy and asked her if she had any suggestions about getting a job. Coincidentally, she had just been promoted and recommended that I apply for her old job.

I wanted to dress the part, but had not owned a suit since I was a young boy taking First Communion. I went to the mall and bought a shirt, jacket, and pants at a store called Express. I felt like the outfit looked sharp, crisp, and professional. In reality, however, I looked more like Tom Cruise in *Risky Business* than a serious businessman.

THE PERFECT INTERVIEW

"How does this look?" I asked my dad. "I need to look professional for my interview."

"Jorgie, what is this outfit?" he asked, barely hiding his disdain. He had always been a great dresser.

"It's Jorge," I said, correcting my father. "I bought it at the mall."

He sighed. "I will help you. Tomorrow, I will show you," he said.

The next day, my father drove me to Brooks Brothers in Century City, just a few miles north of the ice cream outlet he drove me to every Saturday a decade earlier. I wanted to look like a businessman—I wanted to look like my dad—and he was going to teach me how.

My father taught me to always buy shirts with button down collars, to button only the top button on my suit jacket, how to choose ties, and how to use solids and stripes. I realized that I had been an uncoordinated dresser all my life. However, soon I looked conservative and professional in a grey suit, French blue shirt, and butter yellow tie.

I called Cathy's boss, Mike Dodd, at Univest Home Loans and asked for an interview. I dressed in my suit, borrowed my dad's car and went in. I was extraordinarily nervous yet tried not to show it. Mike was sharp and polished. Our interview was a quick one:

Mike: "Have you ever worked in real estate before?"

Me: "No"

Mike: "Any experience with mortgages?"

Me: "No"

Mike: "So, no real estate or mortgage experience whatsoever?"

Me: "No"

Mike: "Perfect."

Mike's assessment came as a surprise. However, he continued on to say that he was looking for someone who was motivated and smart. He did not want candidates with experience, as that meant they already had bad habits that they would need to un-learn. He wanted me green, so he could mold me into his vision. Notably, he didn't even ask if I had any kind of a degree. All I needed was my new real estate license. I realized that all my anxiety before the interview was for nothing. I closed the book on my bike-racing career, accepted Mike Dodd's job offer, and took on my next challenge.

CHAPTER THREE

Loan Originator to Real Estate Mogul

I WAS 24 WHEN I TOOK MIKE DODD UP ON HIS OFFER AND started with Univest Home Loans in February 1990. I was trained as a loan originator, which basically entailed answering an 800-phone number and setting up appointments for those wanting mortgages to meet with a loan officer. To get me started, I was paid $2,000 monthly for the first two months. After that, I was commission only—earning $150 for every appointment I set that turned into a closed loan.

Univest had several branches across California. Borrowers interested in new loans called our central phone room and we scheduled times for them to meet with a loan officer in the nearest office. The first few weeks of calls were anxiety-ridden, as I remained shy, especially when talking to strangers. But I found comfort in the anonymity of the phone.

"These callers are typically going through the Yellow Pages

looking for a loan," Mike explained. He had pulled up his chair next to mine in the phone room.

"Okay," I said, following along intently.

"When they talk to you," he said, "You want to be their last call. You take them off the market."

"Right," I said. "But how?"

"Be professional, welcoming, courteous and knowledgeable," he said. I was scribbling Mike's guidance on a yellow pad.

"I'm fine on the first three," I said, looking up. "But I don't know too much yet about mortgages." In reality, I understood less about mortgages than most of the callers.

"That's fine," he said. "Never guess at answers. Instead, say 'that's a great question, let me check with my supervisor' and put them on hold."

"Okay," I said. "Then I ask my manager?"

"Yes, ask Bruce," he said. "Or anyone who is available. Then, go back with the answer. If you are attentive, respond promptly to phone messages, and are pleasant, you will succeed. People want to do business with people they like."

I closely followed Mike's directives. Within a few weeks, I knew the answers to all the common questions. As some of my appointments started showing up and applying for mortgages, my confidence increased. There were two others in the phone room: my manager Bruce Hale, and another originator, chain-smoking Jim Kelly. The anti-smoking laws had not yet passed and I would often emerge from the phone room with a headache, resulting from hours of inhaling second-hand smoke. The stench and the haze in the room brought back memories of when Smelly Mike stayed at our house.

I was the only one in the room who was unmarried and undistracted by baggage, be it lunch with the wife or kids' soccer games, medical appointments, and all the other responsibilities adults take on as they age. I lived at home and had few responsibilities. Thus, when Bruce or Jim needed to take time off, I always agreed to cover them. Although I was hired to work eight hours a day, eventually I just showed up when the doors opened at 8:00 AM and worked until they closed at 8:00 PM, every day, Monday through Friday. As it had always been, work was my play, my co-workers and the callers were my social outlet, and the ever-growing commission checks were my prizes.

It was a numbers game: the more calls I answered, the more appointments I would set, the more loans successfully closed, and the more money I earned. I brought my food from home in generic Tupperware containers, and then stashed the dishes in my desk drawer so I could graze throughout the day. I would always take small bites, not wanting to get stuck with a mouthful when a call came in. Unlike my co-workers, I didn't have to leave the office to get lunch and dinner. If I had to go to the restroom, I ran there. Within six months, I was closing 30 to 40 deals per month and earning over $5,000 monthly, more than anyone else in the phone room—and even more than my manager.

I took on some of my parents' household expenses, but still had a lot of money left over, which I simply put in the bank. I had found a new game to play: real-life Monopoly with genuine cash. This was fun.

THE FOOTBALL POOL

"Are you going to play the pool this week?" asked Ricardo Starks, a loan officer. He asked me the same question every week. The office had weekly football pools, and most of my co-workers joined in, typically throwing away their money.

"No," I said. "Thanks." I was uninterested in the NFL and the pool. I reasoned that the odds of winning were much worse than the odds that I could schedule the next caller for a loan appointment.

"Come on, you're making good money," Ricardo pressed. "You need to join in." I had withstood the requests to participate in the pool for precisely that reason. I was making real money because I was answering those phones.

"You should play," Bruce Hale said, playfully. "Last week's prize winner got $200."

"I can make $300 closing the next two calls," I thought to myself.

"What American doesn't like football?" asked Jim. "What's the name of L.A.'s NFL team?"

"Raiders," I said, getting annoyed at the friendly pressure. "Okay, here's the deal. I'll put in $20 this one time if you agree to never ask me again."

"Alright," Ricardo said. "Newbery's in the football pool!" He handed me the Xeroxed pool sheet. I didn't know who was better than whom. Whereas Bruce, Jim, and Ricardo and others had carefully calculated their selections, I quickly picked random choices.

I didn't watch the games that weekend. Instead, I went for some long bike rides to clear the office smoke out of my lungs, and went to see Mel Gibson in *Hamlet* with my parents and Anne on Sunday afternoon.

"You won!" said Ricardo when I walked in on Monday morning. He was visibly bewildered as he handed me $200 cash. All my office mates were stunned. "Now, you're going to play every week, right?"

"No way," I replied, surprised at my stroke of luck. "I'm done. I'll go out on top." I reasoned that my win was a fluke and that the chances of a repeat win were slim to none.

"That is so wrong," said Ricardo. They never asked me to join the pool after that. They were too concerned I might win again.

DARIN

As time went on, I continued to set a record pace of closings. In June 1991, a loan officer position became available. One of the company's top men, Roy Leonard, called me into his office near the front of the building. Roy was probably in his mid-50s, chubby with grey hair. He smoked, drank, and looked a bit worn out.

"Jorge, you've been doing good work in the phone room," he said. "Everyone's impressed."

"Thanks," I said.

"There's a new loan officer position opening up," he said.

"I heard about that," I said.

"Darin wants us to make you a loan officer," he said. I was taken aback by his words. Darin Moore was branch manager and the top producer in the whole company. "Frankly, I think you need more experience and that you are too young. All the borrowers will be older than you."

"That's true," I said. I was, after all, only 25. I hadn't interacted much with Darin, but somehow he must have taken note of my diligent follow up and determination. I was pleasantly surprised that Darin had become such an advocate of mine.

"You'll make a good loan officer one day," he said. "I told Darin I would at least offer you the job, but I take it you agree with me and you'll wait a few more years?" I shared in some of

Roy's concerns as I had never been socially comfortable and the thought of in-person interactions as a loan officer created some angst. The phone was a shield that created my comfort zone in the phone room.

"Well," I said, pondering. I was reflecting on the lessons of John Howard, the Olympian who taught me to always look forward.

"Well?" said Roy, sounding a tad impatient. "You're passing on the job, right?"

"I'll take the job," I finally said.

"You sure?" Roy said. He looked surprised and skeptical. He reminded me of Mr. Snodgrass and Chris and the older plump lady at the UCLA Faculty Center; he even reminded me of some of the punks—all of them doubtful of what I could accomplish at my young age.

"I'm sure," I said. I could do this. I would figure this out. "But I have one request."

"What's that?" asked Roy.

"I have worked here for 16 months," I said. "I have never missed a single day. Can I have a week off before I start?" I wanted that week off because I wanted to take a trip with my father.

"Yes, yes," he said. "I'm sure that could be arranged." He looked slightly startled. I'm not sure whether he was still reacting to me accepting the job, or the revelation that I never took a day off in 16 months.

ARGENTINA

"Let's go to Argentina," I suggested to my dad when I got home. My father had left his homeland around 1950 when he came to the U.S. in search of new opportunity. He had since traveled all over the world, but never returned to his native country even though he often talked about Argentina with a great fondness. My father was 71 at the time and had been supporting the family for so many years. Until I asked, I don't think he had contemplated slowing life down a bit to take the opportunity to go back.

"OK, Jorgie," he said. He seemed surprised by my request, but looked happy.

"It's Jorge," I said, correcting my father. "We can go in two weeks."

"Good. I will make calls to let everyone know we are coming," he said, smiling.

A couple of weeks later, accompanied by my brother Alastair, we were touching down at Ezezia, Buenos Aires' international airport. There is also a domestic airport in Buenos Aires named Jorge Newbery Airport, named after my granduncle. He was a pioneering aviator and great risk-taker who died in a ballooning accident. "Newbery has been considered to be the first popular non-political Argentine idol," states Wikipedia. "[He lived] a still-embryonic lifestyle that focused on the development of the body and its potential, exercising self-control and training.

My granduncle, Jorge A. Newbery, a national sports hero in Argentina.

One characteristic of Newbery's personality was the absence of fear; he was known as 'Mr. Courage'."

Soon, we were having tea and dinners with dozens of family members and friends of my father who my brother and I had heard about, yet never met. Buenos Aires is a glorious city, but poorly maintained and crumbling. As we walked the sidewalks, we tried to avoid the ruts and holes in the pavement, along with the dog excrement that appeared to be everywhere. Argentine pet owners had apparently not yet discovered pooper-scoopers.

La Recoleta, the resting place for generations of my ancestors, 1991

My dad shows me around Buenos Aires, 1991

My father took me to La Recoleta, a cemetery in the middle of Buenos Aires, which included a Newbery tomb that looked like a tiny house amongst a whole neighborhood of miniature homes of the dead. His parents and other generations of Newberys were at rest in the tomb. I had never met my grandparents on either side, as my parents married late in life. As we stood outside their house of eternity, I felt a calmness being so close to them. I gave my father a hug, as I realized this was a stirring moment for him. His eyes welled. Mine did too.

I felt thankful in that moment and for the opportunity to travel with my father to his home country. My father rarely showed much emotion, but I could tell that he cherished this visit. He looked reinvigorated and his eyes danced as he shared plans to return again soon. After breaking his 40-year absence, he subsequently traveled back to Buenos Aires frequently. He even bought a small apartment there for his often-extended stays, claiming a home for himself there once again.

LEARNING TO BE A LOAN OFFICER

Upon my return from Argentina, I began my new position as loan officer at Univest. "You need to act like you are confident," Darin counseled. "When you walk into a room, if you look and act confident, people will assume you are. It's all perception."

"Okay," I listened, as I started to underline "ACT CONFIDENT" on my yellow pad.

"If anyone asks you a question you don't know the answer to," he said, "Don't guess. Just excuse yourself and come to ask me."

"Okay," I said, as I underlined "ASK" on my pad.

"Take control of the conversation, answer likely questions before they're asked," he said. I underlined "TAKE CONTROL" on my yellow pad. "Do not approach this as if you are selling anything. They want a loan and you are providing the loan. You have what they want. Help them get it."

"Right," I said. I underlined "HELP PEOPLE" on my pad.

"Also, treat every client the same whether they are looking to borrow $5,000 or $500,000," he said. "Your commission on a $5,000 loan will be tiny, but if you treat that client right, they may come back later for a bigger loan, or refer a friend or family member. Look to the long-term and build relationships."

"Got it," I said. I underlined "BUILD RELATIONSHIPS" on my pad.

"Finally, be friendly and responsive," he said. "People want to do business with people they like." I underlined "BE LIKED" on my pad, and then I crossed it out. I had already learned this from Mike Dodd.

Darin was a great teacher and, as the top producer, he was the one I needed to learn from. To me, he was an Olympian of mortgages and, as with John Howard a few years before, I was the devout student. I absorbed every word of advice, wrote every tidbit down, and reconciled my notes and new knowledge each night at dinner. Just like when I studied books to learn to be a great bike racer, I wanted to excel at real estate and would buy, or borrow from the library, books on real estate and mortgages. I wanted to be the best. I knew I could be.

As prepared as I was, I was still nervous for my first appointment. The mid-50s couple, Delia and Joseph, was looking for a second mortgage to consolidate some high-interest credit cards. I was ready to enter a burn zone. I stepped into the lobby and greeted them, then welcomed them into my office. "ACT CONFIDENT," I thought.

"I understand you are looking for a second mortgage to payoff your credit cards," I said once we all sat down. I was looking into their eyes.

"Yes, we are buried in these cards," Joseph said. "My wife was laid off, and we started charging the cards to keep everything afloat. We've never missed a payment on anything, but it's gotten tough. Delia's back at work now, so we hope you can help get these payments down."

"Here's what we'll do," I said. "Let me ask you several questions and complete an application, then I'll run your credit report and tell you what we can do." "'ASK' and 'TAKE CONTROL'" I thought.

I pulled out a 1003 loan application from my top drawer. I asked every question on each of the four pages. They gave me the answers and I filled them in.

"I just need you to each sign the application," I said, handing them a pen. They signed. "Now, give me a few minutes and I will run your credit report, then we can review."

"Sounds good," said Joseph. They apparently could not tell that this was the first time I'd ever done this. I was doing fine. As I emerged from my office, I made a beeline for Darin's office.

"Darin," I said. "I think I have everything. Can you take a look at the application?" He scanned line by line. After a couple of minutes, he looked up to render his verdict.

"Looks good," he said, smiling. "Now, run a credit report." I went to the computer and ran a TRW report, then matched the debts on the report against what the borrowers had told me. They had underestimated a few, which I learned was common. People tend to underestimate how much debt they actually owe. I then calculated their debt-to-income ratio and determined the loans terms they qualified for on a worksheet

"Darin, can you take a look at my worksheet?" I asked, as I re-entered his office. He took the worksheet, the credit report, and application and reviewed again, checking for consistency and to make sure my calculations were correct.

"This all looks fine," he said. "Go share the good news."

"Here's what we can do," I said once I sat back down in front of Joseph and Delia. I remembered to look them in the eyes. "We can drop your payments by $358 a month by consolidating your credit cards." I watched them both smile hopefully. "'BUILD RELATIONSHIPS' and 'HELP PEOPLE,'" I thought.

I went on to experience great success as a loan officer and, when Cathy left as manager of the City of Industry branch, I was again promoted in her footsteps. In fall 1991, at age 26, I was manager of the City of Industry branch. After only a few months into my promotion, however, I received a phone call and realized that Darin wasn't done pushing his protégé forward.

SUNSET MORTGAGE

"Do you want to start our own mortgage company?" Darin asked me in the winter of 1991.

"Sure," I replied, not having previously considered my next step. Being a branch manager was paying well—I earned over $10,000 on some months, which was fun considering I was still living at home, drove a used diesel car that I had purchased for $2,000 cash, and had no taste for luxury. I was banking most of what I earned.

"Let's meet at Denny's on Saturday morning, okay?" asked Darin. "We'll hash out a plan."

"Sure," I replied. I was looking forward to hearing what he envisioned. I didn't know what exactly to expect, but I looked up to Darin and felt honored that he wanted me to be his partner. He certainly knew others who would be eager to partner with him. As District Rep. Steve Ball appeared to recognize my cycling potential years before, Darin appeared to see something in me as well.

As we chatted at the Denny's on 182nd Street in Torrance directly off the 405 North off-ramp, Darin let me know that Univest was having financial and legal issues and that we should start our own mortgage company. I was intrigued. We agreed to put in $50 each and no more, and to reinvest our earnings into our new company in order to grow.

To have a mortgage company in California, you need to be affiliated with someone with a broker's license. A former Univest appraiser, Bill Boyack, had such a license and he agreed to allow us to work from his Silverlake garage, which was also the headquarters for his appraisal business. Oddly, he had a chicken coop housing maybe a dozen chickens between his home and the garage.

We were unsure what to name our new venture, but as we drove from Silverlake back to Torrance on the Harbor Freeway, we passed Sunset Boulevard. Looking down the street that had been the epicenter of my earlier world, visions of nights at the

Whisky, friendly men in nice cars offering me rides, and the Sunset Riots flashed before me.

"How about Sunset Mortgage?" I proposed.

"That sounds good," Darin said. "Sunset Mortgage it is."

Darin was cautious and calculating, plus he had a wife, two young children, and debt such as a mortgage and auto loans. It understandably left him feeling uncomfortable with the idea of leaving Univest's steady paycheck. As a result, I quit Univest first and soon was working out of the garage behind the chicken coop, which some clients found quite amusing.

The first few loans were done for friends and family, plus Darin referred some loans that Univest rejected as too small or challenging. Our $100 initial investment was soon bolstered by a few loan closings, and we utilized a couple of thousand to incorporate Sunset Mortgage Inc. We had a coin flip as to who would be president. Darin won.

Soon, we had earned enough to start buying ads in the *Los Angeles Times* classifieds and other periodicals to get the word out about Sunset. Then, my sister Charlene started working with me—she worked for free at first, but eventually we were able to pay her a salary.

All was well, except for one noxious issue: Bill was sometimes inconsistent with cleaning the coop, which would reek on hot sunny days. Smelly Mike was an air freshener in comparison. Bill seemed oblivious, as if the funk was just a part of life.

"Bill, I think it's time to clean the coop," I would suggest, striking a helpful tone

"Yes, I'm going to get to it," replied Bill, noncommittally.

"I've got some clients coming over in the morning, so I'd really appreciate it," I added.

"Yeah, sure," said Bill.

However, the morning came and the stench was even worse, permeating my nearby office.

"Ewwww, what's that smell?" asked the client's wife, pinching her nose.

"It's the chickens. Sorry," I replied, terribly embarrassed. "We'll get through the application quickly."

THRILL OF THE DEAL

Within several months, we had earned enough to get a real office. I had also studied for, and passed, the real estate broker's exam. Finally, we could bid *adieu* to Boyack and the rancid chicken coop and say hello to an office on 182nd Street, two blocks from the Denny's where Sunset was first conceived. By 1993, Darin came aboard full time and, as we grew further, we even hired Cathy Hertz, who originally got me into the mortgage business. Around this time, Univest shut down. The declining market had eroded the value of many of their loans, which defaulted, and Univest was awash in legal and financial woes. Sunset picked up some of their clients and employees. We soon grew to a staff of seven.

Sunset was profitable and I used some of my earnings to buy my first rental property: a four-unit apartment building at 424 W. 108th Street in South Central Los Angeles. A few months later, I bought a 19-unit apartment building at 10412 S. Figueroa Street. I kept on buying so that, by 1996, I owned over 500 rental units in Southern California. I managed these with my sister and a small team of trusted employees.

With Sunset, I was 50/50 with Darin. However, I had less personal responsibilities and more time available, so I often devoted a disproportionate amount of time and effort to growing our business. Also, I was the one to always say yes to new loan applications, while Darin would be more prudent and moved more carefully and patiently. I was always swinging for the fences, while Darin earned the nickname "Mr. Small Potatoes."

In retrospect, Darin's conservative nature was a good speed guard for me. He had experienced loss, but I hadn't. He was a few years older than me and had lost money on a few rental properties in the early '90s downturn. We had become good friends and I think he recognized that I had lots of great ideas, but also that I had lots of bad ideas. He also noted that I tended to not appreciate risk. To my credit though, when I made the wrong choice, I took pride in maximizing recovery by working diligently to turn a problem into a solution. However, a more effective strategy would have been to say "no" to the problem deals in the first place.

I learned this lesson when a family from Torrance applied for a second mortgage to consolidate their bills. Our second mortgage interest rate was much lower than their credit cards, so the payment reduced their overall obligations. Still, Darin recognized better than I did that this family was overwhelmed with bills following the husband's unexpected medical expenses. Even though we reduced their monthly payments, they needed to cut their expenses even more. Darin said no, but I insisted. They had a nice home but limited equity, so we loaned 70% of the value of their home instead of the customary 65% for similar credit risks. Darin went along with this, but protested.

The family made their payments on time for over a year and a half, and I found a bit of glee rubbing the payment checks in Darin's face. However, the payments suddenly stopped and the family said that they could not continue. Their bills had buried them. I called and tried to work things out, but they became unresponsive. Their big first mortgage started foreclosure before we did, and the fees and late charges that the first mortgage holder added to the balance quickly eroded the equity protection of our second mortgage. I scrambled for a solution to salvage the investment. The family agreed to move out and a new family agreed to move in, paying us a token payment while they tried to work out a short sale with the first mortgage holder.

Eventually, we lost money on the deal, including most of our $30,000 investment. Darin accurately assessed that I often completed deals just for the thrill of the deal, not so much for what I could earn. The money I earned was just a means to keep score and fuel more deals. He was right.

Excited at doing deals at Sunset Mortgage, 1994

My experiences during this period, whether I won or lost, built a foundation for all my later pursuits. "ACT CONFIDENT," "ASK," "TAKE CONTROL," "HELP PEOPLE," "BUILD RELATIONSHIPS," and "BE LIKED" are the business principles I still utilize today. Looking back, though, providing loans was not always a good way to "HELP PEOPLE." In doing so, I was often a tool of the elite. My perspective has since turned around completely.

RICKY AND THE SPILT COINS

To bolster income at my properties, I installed laundry machines and payphones and even some vending machines. I emptied the cash regularly, even though that meant visiting menacing parts of South Central at all hours. Still, I always treated everyone well and I was generally treated the same.

I remember one day when I had just emptied the laundry and payphone at 10412 Figueroa and the bag of coins that I was carrying to my car burst, scattering hundreds of coins around the sidewalk. There were already several locals hanging out at the liquor store next door, and the sound of the quarters and dimes scattering on the sidewalk promptly drew a crowd, including Ricky, an African American local tough in his early 20s who was shirtless and displaying dozens of what looked like gang tattoos.

I was always friendly and respectful to Ricky—I wasn't afraid of him, and we greeted each other as we would anyone else. He seemed amused by my comings and goings and told me that I looked like a cop. I'm half-Hispanic and half-white, but am typically assumed to be white, and this neighborhood was mostly African American and Hispanic. Not many whites were seen around here except for cops, so I understood his perspective. At least I treated him better than most cops probably did, as Ricky seemed to be in and out of jail regularly.

The coins settled on the sidewalk, glimmering in the sunlight like hundreds of shiny stars on a clear night. About a dozen locals and I surveyed the situation. I envisioned a mass grab for the coins. If just one person had started picking them up, the others would surely have followed in a frenzy like the shoppers on *Supermarket Sweep*. I had been thrust into an unanticipated burn zone, but aid was about to come from an unexpected source.

"Let him pick them up," said Ricky, as he eyed the crowd. I bolted to my truck and pulled another burlap bag from the back. Once I returned, I dropped to my knees to pick up the coins from this sidewalk in a very hardscrabble section of South Central. I was guarded not by the police, but by a frequent target of the police.

"Thanks," I said to Ricky, shaking his hand when I was done as the crowd dissipated. "I really appreciate that."

"No problem, Jorge," he said, appearing to enjoy doing something good. The warmth of our friendly exchanges heightened after this incident. This was proof that people typically treat you the way you treat them—it's human nature, good human nature. The police generally did not treat Ricky and other toughs very well. Hence, these guys reciprocated by blasting NWA's song "Fuck tha Police."

I sometimes wonder what happened to Ricky. Unfortunately, he didn't seem to have many other opportunities to do good for the others in his world. The coins I collected on the sidewalk that day added to my Monopoly money, which I used to buy more buildings and do more deals. By this time, I was spending so much time "playing Monopoly" that I sold my interest in Sunset to Darin and invested the funds to buy more buildings. In doing so, I felt like I was propelling myself forward on a path of my own. Unfortunately, I had given up my speed guard.

THE FORD HOTEL

"Don't buy the Ford Hotel," advised a city health inspector. I had acquired numerous neglected properties and successfully renovated them, turning them into productive and profitable assets. I had to interact with city inspectors on many occasions. They appeared genuinely helpful to me, as I was likely much more responsive than most landlords. "We are going to end up adversarial with you. It's not worth it." The inspector sounded sincere and earnest.

I had set my sights on the Ford Hotel, a 298-unit long term occupancy hotel at 1002 E. 7th Street on Los Angeles' Skid Row. The four prior property owners had all been jailed for slum violations at the hotel. Conditions such as nonworking fire sprinklers, inadequate electricity, rodent infestation, and stopped up plumbing had plagued the hotel for years. Although each successive owner attempted to repair it, the issues were overwhelming and the hundreds of tenants living in the property resulted in new problems popping up as soon as others were fixed.

"You're going to end up in jail," continued the inspector, who was part of Los Angeles' Slum Housing Task Force. In Los Angeles, if you owned a building with slum conditions, under strict liability you were responsible whether you caused the issues or not. This seven-story hotel featured tiny units with only a sink, bed and chair, and a shared bathroom at the end of every hallway, four to a floor. The first owner had acquired the hotel for over $4,000,000 several years earlier, but the price had dropped with each successive sale as each buyer was jailed. I made a deal to buy the hotel for $850,000, an absolute steal. However, I took on the risk of ending up in prison myself. We actually had to send a notary to jail to have the seller sign the deed.

After acquisition, I met with the inspectors and we agreed to a plan: I had six months to complete the work. As long as I was making progress, I would not be prosecuted, provided the project was completed at the end of six months. I went ahead and engaged a crew to start working, clearing out one floor, completing renovations, then moving down to the next floor. The inspectors would visit regularly and were notably impressed with the progress and our cooperation with their requests. I thought everything was going smoothly and everyone was content.

36 CHARGES

"Have you seen the paper?" asked a friend over the phone, just over six months after I purchased the Ford. I had finally moved out of my parents' home and into a condo I had purchased on Chenault near San Vicente in Brentwood, just five minutes from my parents.

"No, why?" I responded.

"You're in it," he responded.

"What does it say?" I asked.

"The headline is '36 Criminal Charges Filed Against Redondo Beach Man'," he said. "Then something about the Ford Hotel. The article is about you." I caught myself holding my breath. I exhaled. I had just finished eating three hardboiled eggs, and the exhale tasted like methane gas. My stomach suddenly felt upset. I had entered a burn zone I did not see coming.

"Hey," I mustered, "Thanks for calling." As soon as I hung up, a vision crackled through my cranium: my mother sitting down for her morning cup of tea and toppling over in her chair when she read this article. Thus, I hastily grabbed my dirty laundry, got into my Isuzu Rodeo, and rushed over to my parents' home.

"Hi Mum. Hi Dad," I said as I walked in through the back door. Both parents were fixing breakfast. I listened for their response, knowing that their voices would indicate if they had perused the criminal allegations against me.

"Hi Jorgie," said my dad, still adding the annoying diminutive "-ie" to the end of my name even though I was now 33. His voice sounded normal, so I was okay for now at least. I dropped off my dirty laundry bag and picked up a bag of clean clothes. My mother still did my laundry, but I don't think she minded. She once did everything for her five children. Now, my remaining needs were laundry and her love and support.

"It's Jorge," I said, correcting my father with what had become an almost automated response.

"Happy New Year's Eve," said my mum.

"*It's going to be happy as soon as I find this paper,*" I thought to myself. "Happy New Year's Eve," I replied as I moved to the dining room. That's when I laid my eyes on what I sought: the unopened *Los Angeles Times*. I rifled through the paper and pulled out the Metro section, which featured the troublesome article. They didn't see me pinch the paper.

"Bye," I said as I grabbed an apple and headed out the door with the offensive pages hidden in my clean laundry.

"Bye, Jorgie," said my parents in unison.

I had completed step one. Step two was to figure out what to do. I needed to consult my attorney, Allan Lowy.

"Hi Allan. This is Jorge. I just read in the paper that the city filed criminal charges against me on the Ford. Please call me back and let me know what to do," I said into his voice mail. This was New Year's Eve, so I reckoned that connecting with Allan was a long shot. I drove to the Ford and went through my workday. I called Allan every couple of hours, but reached his voicemail each time. I didn't leave any more messages, not wanting to appear desperate, even though I was. By 3:00 PM, I realized that I was not going to hear back from Allan until after the holiday. I decided to escape.

ESCAPE

I drove to Los Feliz and Western Avenue, just a few blocks from Studio 9 in the Hollywood & Western building where I had crafted Youth Manifesto sixteen years prior. As I drove, I changed out of my work clothes and into shorts and an athletic top. When I raced bikes, in my eternal pursuit of time efficiency, I had learned to change clothes while driving, maximizing the use of open stretches of freeway and long red lights.

These days, I no longer rode my bike. I was no longer world-class, and riding recreationally was not rewarding. After riding to win for so many years, I had trouble transitioning to riding for fun. Instead, I ran. After I parked on Los Feliz, I tied the laces on my running shoes. My escape was to run the trails up and down the hills of Griffith Park.

The solitude and strenuous effort allowed my mind to reconcile the day and my criminal charges. I had never had any offense greater than a traffic ticket so I was concerned and scared. Maybe I was a little cocky in buying the Ford. Although we had made good progress in the six months, we were not even halfway done. Still, I reasoned that what the city wanted was the building repaired and putting me in jail would deter this. By the end of the run, I had convinced myself that everything would work out. Still, I had trouble thinking about anything else over the long New Year's weekend.

"Jorge, it's Allan," he said by phone. The day was Jan. 4, 1999 and I was in my office at the Ford.

"I am so glad to hear from you," I said. "I've been having trouble sleeping the last few nights." Uncertainty can be most vexing. "Have you talked to the city attorney?"

"Yes," he said. "The city attorney has heard good things from the inspectors. They believe you're making good progress."

"So why'd they file the charges?" I asked, indignant.

"They say they can't selectively prosecute. They had to file the charges," he said. "There are still violations at the property. They know you are working on them, but they jailed four owners already. They can't give you a pass."

"I get it," I said, still agitated.

"These are all housing and health code violations," he said. "But these are criminal charges, so this is serious."

"Ugh," I uttered, in a deep tone. It wasn't a word, just a sound that came out at the thought of going to jail.

"They are willing to make a plea deal," he said. "You plead no contest, pay the city a $10,000 fine and go on two-years' summary probation."

"What's summary probation?" I asked, feeling shattered. No jail was good, but I imagined visiting a probation officer every week.

"Summary probation is the lightest form of probation," he said. "As long as you don't have similar violations at any property in the next two years, nothing happens."

"Do I have to check in every week? I asked.

"No, nothing like that," he said, sounding reassuring.

"Will I have a criminal record?" I asked.

"I talked to the city attorney about that," he said. "If you get all the violations fixed and you get this property signed off, they are open to exonerating you. Then you'd have no criminal record."

"Let's take the deal," I said. Then I let out a long exhale. I didn't taste methane this time. I felt refreshed. "Thanks, Allan." I realized that I might be able to escape after all.

OVER-CONFIDENCE

In October 1999, I let the inspectors know that the project was complete and asked them to inspect it. They advised me that they needed to come out and go through the hotel—and there could not be a single violation. This was no small feat, as the 298-unit building was filled up close to capacity. We had a couple of failed inspections, which were aborted when the inspectors identified issues such as a door closer that would not completely shut a door without assistance. Even seemingly minor things could spell disaster for me.

A couple of days before Thanksgiving 1999, the platoon of inspectors descended one more time. We had spent the last 24 hours checking everything to make sure there was nothing out of order. As they walked in, I broke into a sweat even though the temperature was mild. Sixth floor passed, fifth floor passed, fourth floor passed and on we went. Finally, we reached the basement. As they tested, prodded, measured, and viewed, they could not find a single violation. The inspectors, my contractor, and I all gathered in the basement for a celebratory photo. I had done it. Eight years of slum conditions, four owners jailed, and I was the one to get it right

I had survived another burn zone. If I was borderline over-confident before this, now I felt that I could take on any project, especially those everyone else had failed on. I would be the one to succeed. I shared my brush with the law with my parents. We all laughed when I recounted how I had snatched the Metro section 11 months prior. Within a few months, I signed a contract to sell the Ford for $2,500,000.

I had heard a saying that "the only way to give yourself a chance at massive gains is to expose yourself to massive potential losses." I was willing to take massive risks because I couldn't fathom that I would lose. When I tripped, I would get back up, fix the trip hazard, and keep on running.

CROSSING STATE LINES

The real estate market in Southern California had rebounded, so I found few opportunities for new acquisitions. However, in 1998, I had started brokering REO homes, which are foreclosed homes. My focus was on houses foreclosed by the U.S. Department of Housing and Urban Development (HUD), which I would market to local investors who typically fixed and resold. I likely became the number one HUD REO broker in the country, selling over 600 properties in 1999.

In 2001, flush with cash and now a favorite of lenders, I started looking out of state for new challenges. I went to a HUD apartment building auction in South Dakota, then one in Louisiana. In both cases, the properties sold for more than I felt comfortable paying. I wanted another burn zone to jump into. I felt ready.

PICKWICK

On July 6, 2001, in Kansas City, Mo., I found myself and two others bidding on the courthouse steps for the 233-unit Pickwick Plaza. This 13-story complex represented a formidable challenge for me: a hotbed of drugs, prostitution, and eight deaths in the prior year, four perishing in a deadly blaze and four murdered by what turned out to be a serial killer tenant. One of the bidders dropped out around $700,000, but the other bidder and I went back and forth, back and forth, back and forth.

"$1,400,000," I said. I heard a scoff from the other bidder. He reminded of Chris when I negotiated to buy the ice cream trike.

"$1,400,000 going once, going twice," said the auctioneer. My eyes had met the other bidders'. I was ready to win.

"$1,500,000," the other bidder said. He wasn't smiling. In fact, he looked a bit distraught. $1,500,000 was my pre-determined limit, but he was on the ropes. Our eyes remained locked

"$1,500,000 going once, going twice," said the auctioneer. I thought that if I bid one more time, I could probably knock this guy out. His eyes remained defiant. *"Fuck you, bid one more time. I dare you, asshole,"* is what his eyes were saying. At least that's how I read them.

"$1,600,000," I said. He looked away and shook his head. I smiled. *"Spic, loner, outcast, whatever. I won today,"* I thought.

I just made my plane that afternoon, a flight on the soon-to-be-bankrupt Vanguard Airlines, nonstop to LAX. As I sat down, an elderly gentleman remarked, "You look like you just landed a big job." In many respects, he was right.

FRAZZLED COMMUNITY

Thirty-eight days after the auction, I owned Pickwick. The day I acquired it, we notified all the tenants of a meeting the following evening in the community center. I wanted to let them know what was going to happen. Rumors were already swirling and I wanted everyone to hear the plans from me. Almost a hundred tenants attended, and I shared my plans to rebuild this broken community.

"Do we all have to move?" asked one elderly gentleman. I pledged to repair the complex, get rid of problem tenants and employees, and operate the complex in a professional manner.

"Are you going to do something about all the riff-raff hanging outside at night?" asked a short woman who appeared to be in her 40s wearing a Kansas City Royals T-shirt. "My family and friends get scared visiting me here."

"Everyone can stay," I said. "And we are going to get rid of the nuisances. No more loitering out front."

"Can you have the toilet in my apartment replaced?" asked a woman who appeared to be in her 20s and was wearing large hoop earrings. "It keeps flushing all the time."

"Can you put Corn Nuts in the vending machine?" asked the boy of maybe seven sitting with her.

"Put in the work order for the toilet and we will get it done," I said. "I will talk to the vending machine person about the Corn Nuts and see what I can do. But, no promises on that."

"I have been putting in work orders for months on the toilet," said the lady with the hoop earrings, persistently.

"What unit number?" I asked. "I'll make sure the toilet gets repaired."

In the months prior to my acquisition, conditions at Pickwick had deteriorated so severely that HUD set up a special hotline just to field Pickwick complaints. HUD later told my attorney Allan Lowy that the hotline rang frequently every day until I took over when all the calls finally stopped. We engaged the tenants in our plans, utilized their input, and embarked on cleansing and rehabilitating the brick and mortar and, more importantly, the frazzled community. Even though this was day one, the tenants bought into my vision.

MOVE INTO MAYHEM

Pickwick was my first project away from Southern California. Call me cheap, but I could not justify paying to stay at a hotel while there were dozens of vacant units at Pickwick. Thus, I moved into an apartment at Pickwick and supervised the rehab from the inside. I picked a furnished apartment on the top floor corner, which jutted out a bit from the building. As a result, there were windows on three sides. When I was growing up, my parents always encouraged us to keep the windows open. "The fresh air is good for you," they would say. If the air was cold, we were encouraged to keep the windows open and add a blanket. In fairness, the Midwest got a lot colder than California, so this advice may not have applied in Missouri during the coldest winter months.

In my Pickwick apartment, the windows would be wide-open a dozen stories high. I felt like I was living in a bird's nest, with a swirl of air soothing my body every night. The unit was sparse, but clean. This was a studio, a single room with a bed, chair and desk, a kitchenette, and a bathroom. It was all I needed. Besides, the majority of my time was spent downstairs in my office.

Although living in my projects was driven by thriftiness, the willingness to move into the mayhem was lauded by the media as exemplifying my significant personal commitment to these rehabilitation efforts. It shattered the image of a typical out-of-town owner who visited the property infrequently and stayed at the Hyatt while their tenants lived in squalor.

BARRED BOOK

My turnaround plans for Pickwick were formulaic and followed the same script as the Ford Hotel. With 12 stories, we emptied a floor, rehabbed all the units, then moved tenants in from the lower floors and repeated on the next floor. Problem tenants were encouraged to leave as we restricted after-hours visitors, started evictions, and cooperated with the police to rid the building of nuisances. Police get frustrated with challenged buildings where arrests are not followed by evictions—and we made sure to do better. Many landlords are happy simply collecting rent, regardless of the negative impact on neighbors that a nuisance tenant can create.

We manned the front desk 24-hours every day and required ID for all guests. Coupled with cameras on all floors, we could track who went where. Anyone arrested or otherwise causing trouble was entered into a "Barred Book." There were over 200 individuals barred from entering Pickwick. We made life uncomfortable for troublemakers and some nuisance tenants left voluntarily. For others, if we could document illegal activity such as drugs and prostitution, we would evict.

Within six months, Pickwick was transformed and positive word of mouth attracted higher-income tenants who would never have considered living there before. Soon, we were close to capacity and, by late 2002, I was further emboldened and on the hunt for another challenge—the more problematic, the better. I soon found what would become my life's greatest challenge.

CHAPTER FOUR

My Debt Drama: Hero to Zero

THOUGHTS OF REGRET SOMETIMES WAFT THROUGH MY mind. I try to promptly dispel these, as I know it is better to look forward. Nevertheless, as I look back at my life and the roads I have chosen, there is one choice that causes me the most heartache: buying Woodland Meadows, an 1,100-unit apartment complex in Columbus, Ohio. This was one of the largest apartment complexes in the country and was to be the flagship of my ever-expanding empire. Instead, this flagship turned my life into a cow chip.

"There are no problems, only challenges," I was fond of saying as I led my team through the chaos that engulfed Woodland Meadows. In retrospect, though, we really did have problems.

I have never fully recovered—rather it feels like I suffer from a wound that keeps reopening. My mind is still a little shaken, less secure than before, less confident, with a feeling that whatever

I build up now could easily be torn down. More than a decade of successfully turning around troubled properties did not prepare me for what transpired at Woodland Meadows. My eternal optimism served me well through hundreds of other projects, but ended up fueling my spectacular downfall. I felt close to shattering a few times. I did not break, but I wore thin during my debt drama.

CHAGRIN BEGINS ON CHAGRIN

"I'm in Kobe's league now," I exclaimed to pal Brad Gerszt over my cell phone as I exited the Hilton Easton on Chagrin Drive in Columbus. This was November 2002 and I had just won Woodland Meadows, an 1,100-unit apartment community, at bankruptcy auction for $12.5 million. The property was the largest single plot of land in the city of Columbus and well located, backing into the exclusive Bexley neighborhood and situated near Columbus' main airport. However, the property was nicknamed Uzi Alley, a tribute to the gangs, prostitutes, guns, and drugs contaminating the complex.

"Kobe" was referring to Kobe Bryant, the Los Angeles Lakers' star who embodied success in my hometown of Los Angeles. I was not much of a Lakers fan, instead finding myself rooting for the lowly Clippers, repeating a lifelong pattern of identifying with the underdog. Still, in this moment, I felt like I belonged in Kobe's class.

Since acquiring my first four-unit apartment building a decade earlier, I had progressed to larger and more challenging targets. I was determined to go bigger and bigger, and backed up

"Rent From Us" T-shirts—part of our early marketing efforts to attract some of Columbus' booming Hispanic population. My father later advised me that my Spanish translation was incorrect.

my aspirations with smarts and an indefatigable work ethic. I closed my purchase of Woodland Meadows on Dec. 31, 2002, and then set out employing the same strategies as the Ford Hotel and Pickwick. Step one was to move into the model unit above the office, otherwise known as my move into mayhem.

EMPOWERED RESIDENTS = EMPOWERED COMPLEX

Woodland Meadows was massive: 1,100 units in 122 three-story buildings sprinkled across 52 acres of winter-dead grass and bare trees. Even at 50% occupancy, due to poor maintenance and poorer management, there were well over a thousand residents. Woodland Meadows was like a small city with John Gregory as the unofficial mayor.

John was a former Woodland Meadows resident and a proud father of seven, but he acted as a father-figure to hundreds of the low and moderate-income residents, who were predominantly African American, like John. He was maybe 5' 10", stocky, with a wide smile. He founded The Enrichment Association of Community Healing (TEACH), a faith-based nonprofit which provided services to Woodland Meadows' residents and others in the community. Some ignored him, especially the troublemakers, but others sought his help and guidance.

When I first toured the complex as part of my pre-auction due diligence, I encountered John and some of his associates behind the TEACH building at the center of the complex. The prior owner had allowed TEACH free use of the building, likely recognizing the benefits that the services provided to residents. John was rightfully concerned about the auction and TEACH's future. Presumably, a new owner could terminate TEACH's use of the building and displace John and his program. Wisely, John had aligned himself with another bidder who promised John an active role in the property's future. However, this bidder had trouble getting their deposit check and arrived to the auction too late to bid. Thus, the paths of John and I were destined to cross. John recounts our first meeting in January 2003:

Jorge was walking in the community and somebody who

*worked for me at the time bumped into him and they said,
"You got to come meet my boss."*

*And so they brought Jorge in and, with his sarcastic humor,
we met. We laughed and talked a little bit, and then Jorge
came back and asked me to do some projects for him for free.*

*The first project he asked me, he said, "I've got these people.
We've got to go collect rent. Can you go do that?" I was like,
"Sure." And so we went to collect some rent for him or at least
let him know where people were.*

*And then he came back the next week. He said, "Hey, I got
another project for you." Free again. We did that project.
Did a good job.*

*And then he came back and I was like, "Dude, we will not
be doing any more free projects for you."*

He said, "No, no. I want you to come work with me."

A few days later, John was the manager of Woodland Meadows.
On his first day, we started off in my office discussing ideas and
strategies. John was seated in front of my desk.

"Get rid of the security," John suggested, appearing both genuine
and sincere in his desire to improve Woodland Meadows. "The
officers are provoking some of the drama on these streets."

"Are you sure?" I replied. I, too, was troubled by the security.
They reminded me of the disciplinarians of my past: Catholic

nuns and the cops at the Sunset Riots. Woodland Meadows' security was comprised of a dozen white adrenaline-fueled rent-a-cops, all armed. They appeared to always be looking for excuses to bop some heads. Worst of all, there was actually a holding cell in the basement of the administrative building. Detained suspects, almost always African-American, were sometimes placed in the cell until the real police arrived. I was surprised that this was legal and advised security to stop using the cell as soon as I took over.

"Who is going to replace them?" I asked, intrigued.

"You, me, the residents," said John. "We'll have a Community Patrol." I sat back in my chair and stared at the ceiling, contemplating the situation. We were paying a dozen full-time officers, yet we had one of the highest crime rates in the city. Something had to change. I looked at John.

"Let's try the Community Patrol," I said. "If everything goes well, I'll lay off the security force next week."

Soon, John and I were patrolling Woodland Meadows' 52 acres at all hours of the day and night. This was at the very beginning of our efforts to cleanse the criminal elements from the community. Our goal was to make the complex safer and more hospitable for the majority of the tenants, who were typically poor and simply trying to scrape by.

"You can't hang on the corner," John would bellow as we walked up on a group of young men on a corner. "You need to step off the property." I had already heard from residents about their discomfort when throngs of mostly African American males were huddled up in front of buildings and on corners. They didn't feel safe and neither did their friends or family when they came to visit.

"We're stepping," replied the group, as they walked away. However, they typically reappeared elsewhere on the property in short order. These men were residents, children, relatives of tenants, or baby daddies to many of the single mothers who lived at Woodland Meadows.

"We got your license plate number," John shouted to a businessman beckoning a young female into his car. The car squealed off.

"I needed that scratch," complained the young lady, sounding irate.

On weekends, johns and drug users would line up for treats, reminiscent of when my dad and I queued up in that line of ice cream trucks almost 25 years before. This go around, though, I wanted the treats to melt.

John stepped right into uncomfortable situations, interrupting drug sales, scaring off johns, and breaking up crowds gathered on corners. These were opportunities for John to evangelize, pressing troublemakers to stop "doing dirt," and to embark on more positive pursuits. John would even invite them to Sunday church services, held at the TEACH building.

A week later, I was convinced that the unarmed Community Patrol was the better solution. I terminated Woodland Meadows' security force, employees that I inherited as part of my acquisition. Much like the punks rioted in reaction to the imposing police build up outside the T.S.O.L. concert two decades before, there was logic in removing the agitator, in this case the white security guards, and replacing them with residents that had a genuine desire to improve their community. John and I were the first patrolmen, and we soon recruited Michael Wilson, who recollected in a 2014 interview:

> *Woodland Meadows was—when Newbery came—it was probably the worst area in the city. Before Newbery left, the crime went down 62%. I know because I was head of the Community Patrol. We'd hit the door at the dope spots and say, "Hey, man, you got to shut this down for real." I was able to do that because Newbery gave me the authority to do it. I was given the opportunity to go to court and testify. "I'll shut you down. If you don't want to live and do right, I'll be the one that will come to court and say, 'Hey, this person is incorrigible.'" I learned some new words. "You're incorrigible."*

John elaborated:

> *I mean there were some people we had to have the police help them off the property. But for the most part, the people in the community kind of took responsibility themselves. They wanted to be a part of the change. I think that that's the story: if you give people responsibility for their own destination, they will step up and take it. So they saw that somebody cared. Jorge cared. Then, they saw that there was some positive action going on, and they stepped up.*

Frustratingly, though, the opportunities for a felon with few work skills living at Woodland Meadows were very limited. Although words were inspirational, there were few resources available for a drug dealer on the corner who decided to go straight. After being turned down for jobs at McDonald's, Arby's, and Wal-Mart, a Woodland Meadows resident may have believed that their only option was to go back to the corner to deal or trick. Dollars were needed for rent, food, and other necessities—it was an inescapable reality.

John proposed that we hire contractors who would teach skills to residents and hire them for labor and apprentice work. I agreed and we invited residents, especially the troublemakers, to a two-week class with the promise of paying jobs upon graduation. Prospects would first learn soft skills, and then work training. The participants' first test was to simply show up every day on time, dress appropriately, listen, and learn.

Few showed up at first, but as word of mouth spread that the graduates were really receiving paying jobs, the classes were soon at capacity. Men and women of all races participated, and shirts, slacks, and even neckties soon replaced baggy pants. The energy of the program proved infectious, not just for participants but also for speakers whom had a captive audience determined to learn. Contractors, politicians, and business people started joining in, sharing stories, struggles, and lessons to inspire the class members.

The first graduates became part of the contractor crews renovating units at Woodland Meadows. The work by these graduates proved to be of good quality, comparable or better than I saw at my other complexes. Notably, the walls these crews were painting were no longer tagged and the apartments they renovated were no longer vandalized, as the former taggers and vandals were now the ones doing the work. Murderers, thieves, drug dealers, and prostitutes all had the opportunity for a fresh start. The success was not 100%, but the impact was. The progress of the program brought to mind a maxim from eBay founder Pierre Omidyar: "Give someone the right tools and the benefit of the doubt, and they'll rarely screw you."

The program soon expanded to all facets of Woodland Meadows employment and, in short order, construction crews and office staff were made up in large part by residents who had gone through the TEACH program. I got to know many of them well. The millions of renovation dollars spent on the property were now, in part, being earned by residents; they were then better able to pay rent and support their families. Empowered residents = Empowered complex.

Taking this a step further, some of the residents soon started forming their own companies and providing lawn care, carpet cleaning, and other services to the complex and to other local businesses. Some positive media reports on the program helped attract other businesses willing to hire TEACH graduates and support the efforts. Ironically, Arby's may not have been willing to employ Joe the felon who lived at Woodland Meadows. However, Arby's was willing to hire Joe's Lawn Service, owned and operated by Joe the felon who lived at Woodland Meadows.

I recalled Ricky, who stood guard over my spilled coins on Figueroa Street several years prior, and how he might have thrived in the TEACH program. Sadly, millions of young African American men like Ricky do not get TEACH-like opportunities. John was the ringleader of the program and I am sure he enjoyed witnessing his vision become reality and the positive impact this work had on hundreds of lives. I was glad to be a part of the success of the TEACH program, which benefitted Woodland Meadows from both social and business perspectives.

Looking back, no big company could have accomplished what we achieved at Woodland Meadows. This was due in large part to the fact that their actions rarely fall in step with the narrative they try to present. People always recognize when they are being sold a story and when someone is genuine. We engaged hundreds in our cause, which was for the benefit of all. We succeeded because we were transparent and we were sincere. My drive came from the challenge of prevailing where others had failed.

Hard-working TEACH crew members taking a break

Soon, Franklin County was encouraged enough to issue $13,500,000 in tax-exempt bonds to refinance my higher interest rate construction debt. Stephen Peterson, a bond portfolio manager from the investment arm of Allstate Insurance, visited the complex and agreed to buy all the bonds. Success bred success and new doors kept opening.

As word of our achievements traveled, I was presented new opportunities to turn around similarly challenged complexes in Indiana, Michigan, Oklahoma, elsewhere in Ohio, Texas, and other states. My portfolio soon grew to 4,000 units across the country. Still, Woodland Meadows was by far the largest and highest profile. No other company leader would have integrated themselves so completely into the fabric of Woodland Meadows. The risk was too great, not only financially, but also personally. Some risks you cannot anticipate.

I am joined by City Councilwoman Charleta Tavares, and John Gregory at the Get Out The Vote rally at Woodland Meadows in fall 2004

Mayor Michael Coleman, on right, schmoozing for votes at Get Out The Vote rally, Woodland Meadows, 2004

Leading a group of children at Woodland Meadows, 2004

CHRISTMAS 2004: LIGHTS GO OUT

Santa missed me at Woodland Meadows in 2004. I thought that I had been good—in the prior two years, I had helped turn around this massive complex with the help of an army of tenants and ex-felons. It sounds cliché, and maybe I was naïve, but I was trying to do well by doing good. And we were having an impact. Hundreds of predominantly young African American men had proven to themselves and everyone else that, given the opportunity, they could excel. There were alternatives to doing dirt, and these guys were maximizing their chance.

As residents took heed of Mahatma Gandhi's insight: "You must be the change you wish to see in the world," the perception of Woodland Meadows changed, both for residents and the surrounding community. Instead of a danger zone to be avoided, Woodland Meadows represented a hope zone, a beacon to others seeking affordable housing and a welcoming community. We were filling new units as fast as they were completed.

Sometimes the transformation was manifested in modest conquests: Before I took over, none of the local pizza companies would deliver to Woodland Meadows. Several months later, Domino's, Papa John's, and other delivery cars were regularly zipping through the complex. To spread the word, we even bought airtime on the local UPN affiliate to broadcast commercials to attract new tenants. When a Southwest Airlines flight attendant moved in, I knew we had crossed a threshold. I didn't think anything could stop us.

Our efforts to resurrect Woodland Meadows bore so much fruit that we even had a Christmas party that year for the many who had contributed to the community's tremendous shift, including employees, contractors, crews, and TEACH program graduates. We rented a nearby hall and over a hundred attended, reveling in a shared optimism that we were all part of something bigger. What had started as a flash at Woodland Meadows was now maturing to a steady glow. People started believing the vision that a community hobbled by neglect, crime, and chaos could be reborn as an asset to the community. We had done it, but as we partied in mid-December, none of us could fathom that one of the angels on the Christmas tree was the Angel of Death.

The party included dinner, then a DJ and dancing after. I flashed back to school dances and my awkwardness and nonexistent rhythm. I tried to stay engaged in conversations far from the dance floor.

"Mr. Newbery," said Deveonne Gregory, John's daughter who worked at Woodland Meadows. "Do you want to dance?"

"No," I said. "Thanks."

I was enjoying the company, but there was no way I was going to get out on that dance floor.

"Mr. Newbery," said Kira, who worked reception and had a snake tattoo running up her neck. "Do you want to dance?"

"No," I said. "Thanks."

Everyone on the floor looked like they were enjoying themselves. However, they all looked like such good dancers.

"Mr. Newbery," asked Roberta Grooms, who worked with TEACH. "Do you want to dance?"

"No," I said. "Thanks."

A few minutes later, I started hearing some murmuring from Deveonne, Kira, Roberta, and a gaggle of other females all clustered in a corner of the dance floor. The haunting piano/drum intro of Akon's "Locked Up" started flowing from the speakers, then the lyrics began:

> *I'm steady tryna find a motive*
> *Why do what I do?*
> *Freedom ain't getting no closer,*
> *No matter how far I go*

The volume of the cackling started to increase. I glanced over and beheld the throng of females heading my way. There must have been 15 of them. *"No,"* I thought.

> *My car is stolen, no registration,*
> *Cops patrolin and now they done stop me,*
> *And I get locked up*

"Mr. Newbery," said Deveonne, the apparent ringleader. "We all decided that you are going to dance with us."

"Please," I begged. "I don't want to dance." I was smiling outside, but petrified inside.

"Come on, Mr. Newbery. You're going to dance," said Kira, grabbing my hand. Deveonne clasped my other hand. They started pulling me. "It'll be fun."

Can't wait to move forward with my life,
Got a family that loves me and wants me to do right
But instead I'm here locked up

"No, please," I pleaded. The only dancing I ever enjoyed was in the slam pits in my punk days.

"Come on, Mr. Newbery, dance," chimed in the others.

They won't let me out, they won't let
*   me out, (I'm locked up)*
They won't let me out, they won't let
*   me out, (I'm locked up)*
They won't let me out, they won't let
*   me out, (I'm locked up)*

I could now feel the soft wood of the dance floor beneath my feet. All the girls started dancing. I had no choice. I had been pulled into a burn zone that I was woefully unprepared for. I took a deep breath. "*I can do this,*" I thought to myself. I moved my arms like I was running at a modest pace, and started moving my feet, repeating a short step in and out.

As I closed my eyes, I thought of John Travolta in *Saturday Night*

Fever, a big hit when I was a kid. Then, I opened my eyes and looked down at my body's ebb and flow with the beat. Suddenly, I realized that I was dancing more like Shaggy in *Scooby Doo*. I had gained no rhythm in the last three decades.

"Please end soon," I pleaded with Akon. Everyone else looked like they were having fun dancing, but I was tortured. As soon as the song ended, I exited the dance floor. I sat down at a table with some of the male TEACH workers and soon was engaged in a lively conversation on what we all planned for 2005. My dance floor torment had subsided, but I had no idea that true agony awaited.

On Christmas Eve 2004, a Friday, I was in Los Angeles spending time with my parents and siblings when John called. "There was a really bad ice storm here last night and the power is out, it's below zero outside, and the heat's not working," he blurted in an angst-filled voice. "The lights are out to like half of Columbus, even the mayor's house has no power. The property is really messed up, too. Trees down all over. With the holiday, it's tough to get any workers out."

Although John sounded alarmed, I stayed calm and imagined that this was merely another speed bump. We had cleared several in the last two years at Woodland Meadows, so cresting one more and staying on track seemed plausible at the time. I did not grasp the gravity of the disaster that had struck.

"John, do whatever you need to in order to keep things going," I said. "I'll be back on Sunday, so we can figure it out then. Remember: there are never problems, only challenges. Merry

Christmas." I was relaxing, at least relatively. Somehow, I always felt the need to exceed and this relentless drive rarely allowed me permission to unwind. Nevertheless, the resurrection of Woodland Meadows was a conquest that was extremely gratifying to complete, so I was able to let up the pressure on myself momentarily.

"Merry Christmas to you too, but be prepared when you get back. It's really bad out here," ended John. You can hit me with terrible news and my reaction is always the same: I do not react impulsively, and I allow my mind to calmly weave a solution. My brain thrives on solving problems, and I enjoy the adrenaline rush of putting together puzzles while under a deadline. I did not interpret the news of the storm damage as overly dire. If the power was out to half of Columbus, I reasoned that city and power company crews were likely working towards a prompt restoration. The property owner is typically not involved in restoring power during a blackout.

As I lay in bed that night, the potential impact started searing into my brain. *"Wait, if there's no power and it's below zero and we have over 900 units occupied, a lot of families were freezing at Woodland Meadows."* All while I was in a warm bed in California. It didn't seem fair. I did not sleep well that night.

Typically optimistic that nothing bad was ever going to happen, I had opted for a high deductible of $250,000 in order to reduce Woodland Meadows' annual insurance premium. Thus, for damages under $250,000, the insurer would pay nothing.

"Do you think there's enough damage to file an insurance claim?"

I asked John, now back in my office on the second floor of the administration building at Woodland Meadows the Monday after Christmas. "When I was running this morning, I saw a lot of trees down and some were on power lines. There's tons of snow out there too, but it looked calm."

Snow can soften even the hardest edges. As I ran, I could not help but admire the drifting snow blanketing the expansive grounds dotted with dozens of mature trees, although some were felled by the storm. That day, Woodland Meadows looked like a nature park. The wounds of the ice storm were camouflaged beneath the pristine snow.

"We had lots of calls from tenants over the weekend, and all the workers are out there surveying units now to try to get heat back on," said John.

To the exasperation of some freezing tenants, we were able to get the water and heat promptly restored to the administration offices and my apartment due to relatively modest damage. Hundreds of families did not have hot water, so we let many tenants shower in my apartment. Some tenants even slept in my apartment. The scene brought back memories of punks in sleeping bags strewn around my parents' living room. However, this time my mother was not around, so the tenants fixed their own breakfast.

The administration office grew akin to a triage center in a war. *Figure out who needs what and get it to them, prioritize the most urgent situations.* I handed out my credit card to rent hotel rooms and purchase hundreds of electric space heaters. Soon, the Red Cross opened a disaster recovery center at the church across the street.

I prepared an email to Neal Novak of Sill & Company, a public adjuster who had represented Woodland Meadows in a fire insurance claim earlier in 2004: "Neal - We had a severe ice storm last Thursday and most of the power was not restored until Sunday. Trees are down all over the place and the boilers are still not working, so there's still no heat. Can you send someone out to see if there is enough damage to file an insurance claim?"

Novak sent out Michael Werner to survey the property two days later. The temperatures had risen and some of the frozen pipes started to thaw. This initially appeared to be good news, but soon pipes all across the property started bursting and flooding apartments.

The insurer had sent out an adjuster who was surveying a dry apartment when a pipe exploded, spraying water like a geyser and rapidly flooding the apartment. He promptly left and said he needed to send someone more senior out. However, no higher-up returned.

Instead, the insurer sent back word that the damages were not covered because we did not have a boiler endorsement, which covers damages caused by faulty boilers. However, the state had inspected and signed off on our boilers in October, less than three months before. The chaos was not the result of faulty boilers, but rather a natural disaster that cut power to the boilers, which then froze and, in many cases, cracked. The insurer was simply looking for an excuse not to pay the claim, which I later found out is very common. A cracked boiler is like a cracked engine head in a car—the damage is fatal.

Sill recommended that we hire Belfor, an international disaster remediation company. Soon, Brandon Carr from Belfor showed up with a young provocatively dressed female assistant. Brandon seemed professional and his assistant was friendly, although she was displaying what seemed like an inappropriate amount of cleavage. I signed the contract.

We were covered for over $40 million in insurance, which was split in three: one insurance company, Chubb, was responsible for the first $2.5 million in damages, another company was responsible for the next $2.5 million, and then reinsurance kicked in and the claim needed to be approved by Lloyds of London. Belfor got moving, believing that the insurers would pay for their work.

Truckloads of equipment and battalions of workers soon arrived at Woodland Meadows. Rows of generators, temporary heaters, and drying equipment hummed 24/7 in order to mitigate the damages. For the tenants, and me, the scene was awesome due to the sheer volume of activity and machinery. The sight was comforting too because it appeared that recovery was achievable soon.

Not wanting the professional contractors to come in and quash our ambitious TEACH crews, I required that Belfor hire the TEACH workers to incorporate into their crews. Despite the early theatrics about the damage not being insured, Belfor appeared deft at working with the insurers. Soon, Chubb paid out their full $2.5 Million, which provided a cash injection which helped get everyone moving.

Although the initial progress was slow as the weather was frequently uncooperative, Woodland Meadows was soon stabilized. Generators were pumping heat into the veins of the frozen buildings. Crews were extracting the water that had drowned units. Other wounds were being addressed as well, such as trees that had fallen onto roofs and ceilings that had caved in. Although our situation was no longer critical, the contractors forecast a long, challenging road to recovery.

"It was just a freaking mess," said Stephen Peterson of Allstate, Woodland Meadows' bondholder, in a 2014 interview. "It's not just the building problem. It's a people problem. People who were living there, it's the middle of winter and the apartments were frozen, and no electricity and so that was a real crisis, a human crisis."

17 DAYS

"Did you see the paper?" John Gregory was asking on almost a weekly basis. The Columbus Dispatch had written a few positive articles on Woodland Meadows when I first took over, sharing pleasant surprise that I had actually moved into the complex. However, reporter Barbara Carmen, who reported that she grew up at Woodland Meadows years before, seemed intent on finding fault with our efforts. Even in Woodland Meadows' greatest hours in 2004, Barbara would ignore hundreds of satisfied tenants to find a handful who were unsatisfied, and then she would gleefully crucify us. In an 1,100-unit complex, she knew if she knocked on enough doors, she was certain to find a unit with roaches.

We had routine extermination service at all the buildings, but some tenants' housekeeping was not very good and this attracted ants and insects, which would then invade neighbors' units. Further, if a leak occurred upstairs and caused damage to the unit below, residents often did not report the issues until the problem was bigger and more expensive to fix. We preached preventive maintenance, as catching small problems early is better for everybody. Still, although most residents bought into our utopian vision, there were always some who liked to keep their view dim. It seemed that Barbara always found those exceptions.

No matter what progress we made, she was intent on derailing us. Her extraordinarily negative approach was hard to grasp. This wasn't just churning out bad news to sell papers—there was more going on here, although I wouldn't learn what it was until years later. As our team was scrambling to recover from the storm, the Dispatch was jeering us from the sidelines, throwing mud at us in our weakest moment:

> "...The Woodland Meadows apartment complex is a massive slum...The pre-Christmas ice storm that bombed the city is to blame...

It was only 17 days after what was the largest federally-declared disaster in Ohio history. With 122 buildings on 52 acres, Woodland Meadows likely suffered the greatest single loss:

"Residents streamed into the community center at the complex to find help, but most didn't want to move out. They have found here a sense of community and appreciate Newbery's management, which they say cares. But love is no substitute for competence. It's time for elected officials to demand accountability."

Barbara's criticism kept flooding in, offering a perspective stemming from thinly veiled personal bias and presenting itself as objective reporting.

"Let's face it. This car is totaled."

She was in attack mode, charging ahead in a way that made it seem like this was the opportunity she had been waiting for.

"Should the owner fail, like the others before him, I suggest buying out investors and bringing in bulldozers. Sell most of the land for development and invest the profits to build decent, rent-subsidized apartments. In 2001, (Mayor) Coleman established the Affordable Housing Trust Fund to lure developers to build housing for the poor. Here's his chance to show off how smart he was."

Why was the *Dispatch* foretelling our demise just 17 days after we were shattered by this massive catastrophe, and scorning the efforts of hundreds of residents and skilled tradesmen feverishly piecing us back together? What was expected of us after 17 days? If she had researched other disasters, she would have found that recoveries are measured in several months and even years, not 17 days. Why was this happening? Thoughts were swirling through my mind: *Maybe we moved slower than we should, maybe we needed more help, maybe we were not doing our best, maybe we weren't as good as we thought? I thought people liked me. I thought people liked us.*

I felt like I was trying to bail out flooded basements while the *Dispatch* had lined up a battalion of water cannons on James Road, intent on drowning any hope of recovery. The bad press spooked neighbors, investors, lenders, and other stakeholders. Malcolm X once warned, "If you're not careful, the newspapers will have you hating the people who are being oppressed, and loving the people who are doing the oppressing." The *Dispatch* was changing the discourse: instead of speculating as to how soon Woodland Meadows would recover, the speculation became how soon Woodland Meadows would die. Only 17 days had passed since disaster struck, yet the *Dispatch* was already writing Woodland Meadows' obituary.

"On my own, I faced a gang of jeering in strange streets," I recalled The Clash's words. "When my nerves were pumping and I fought my fear in, I did not run. I was not done." I would not run. I was not done. But coming out on the other side would take me to places I would have never thought I'd find myself in.

MY FIRST VISIT TO A STRIP CLUB

I made it 39 years of my life without stepping foot in a strip club. Call me a prude, and that may be true, but I was more interested in healthy living and exploring my physical and mental limits than drinking and leering at girls. Strip clubs are not components of a successful athlete's lifestyle. Neither are drugs, unless you are Lance Armstrong. Today, I am a runner and still win races, besting runners half my age. Choosing a lifestyle that includes strip club avoidance has advantages.

"Here's the address of where we are meeting with Belfor," advised my trusted employee Crystal Sessley. Belfor was regularly entertaining the insurance adjusters at swanky restaurants and seedy strip clubs in order to coax them to increase their damage repair costs high enough to cover Belfor's inflated billings. This certainly was not my style, but they convinced me that this is how it is done.

As I have aged and lost my naiveté, I found that this "entertaining" is commonplace in big business. Some days, it seemed that Belfor management spent more time in bars and strip clubs than they did supervising the restoration. Crystal knew me well enough to know that I would not go to a strip club. Thus, she simply gave me the address, which I presumed was a restaurant where we would meet. She wisely did not mention the nature of the venue.

The place was nondescript on the outside and did not have the telltale neon "GIRLS, GIRLS, GIRLS" signs you sometimes see. Besides, I was running late and was not paying much attention. However, when I stepped in and they asked for a cover charge, I quickly realized that my strip club abstinence was about to end.

"He's with us," Brandon Carr, our main Belfor contact, said as he waved me in with his right hand. His left was in the hand of a completely naked young lady trailing behind him. Brandon was probably my age, white, with dark hair. If I saw him on the street with this young lady, I would have assumed that they were father and daughter. She looked to be 20 years old at the most, probably 6 feet tall in bare feet, long-legged and lean, with shoulder-length blond hair.

"You can go in," said the attendant.

"Glad you made it," said Brandon, shaking my hand.

"Thanks," I said. I was not sure what I was thanking him for, but I guess it was because he took care of my cover charge.

"We're at a table over here," he said. I followed him and his acquaintance. She had a tattoo right at the base of her back: Miss Kitty sitting on a flowering vine. It seemed out of place. As we passed several other all-nude girls, I blushed. However, I noticed that these young women were nothing like the glistening Demi Moore in *Striptease*. Instead, many looked painfully thin and unhealthy—drugs, alcohol, and/or hard living must have dulled the polish. The décor was like the girls: a cheap attempt at classy. The furniture setup was reminiscent of Olive Garden, but the decorations were more Chuck E. Cheese.

These grown men were acting like kids at a birthday party. I sat at the table, but no business was being discussed as I had anticipated. Instead, these older lecherous guys were ogling and groping these troubled young girls, having them sit in their laps, and do who knows what else once they walked to the private rooms. The whole scene seemed dirty to me.

Maybe that's how the world works, but it is just not what I am accustomed to. Brandon kept offering to pay girls to go to a private room with me. It was easy to say no, again and again. He was trying to be a gracious host, and I tried to hide my annoyance. I promptly left. I am now 49, and this remains my one and only strip club visit.

EYE CANDY

Belfor's strategy to maximize the insurance claim was to pleasure the insurance adjusters. I discovered that the provocatively dressed Belfor employee who visited Woodland Meadows immediately after the ice storm was previously a strip club employee. That's fine, except that my insurance claim likely included a hefty salary to her for doing little more than being eye candy for Belfor management.

Strip clubs or not, Belfor's strategy was not working well. Anticipating reimbursement by the insurers, Belfor was billing their Woodland Meadows work at very high rates. I guessed this was necessary to cover the philandering expenses. However, the insurance company balked at paying what was escalating into a very substantial claim. As a result, we filed a lawsuit against the insurer, RSUI. The insurer had released some funds, but the bondholders were refusing to release these out of concern that the funds were insufficient to complete the project.

Optimistic that the insurance claim would eventually be paid in full, I borrowed heavily on my other properties in order to rebuild Woodland Meadows. However, the damage was immense and, despite pouring millions into the effort, I ran out of funds by summer.

Without the funding to continue, Belfor and other contractors abandoned the project. In the interim, the city had asked us to meet weekly to update them on the restoration progress. Although we had small crews making modest progress, we were running on financial fumes—basically whatever cash I could cobble together each week.

In September 2005, I asked my friend Verria Kelly to move from St. Louis to Columbus to help out at Woodland Meadows. She took residence in an apartment below mine in October 2005. Verria was almost three years younger than me, African American, attractive with a ready smile. A mutual friend had introduced us less than a year before. Verria was interested in investing in real estate and I coached her. Then she explained that she wanted to sell her home and leave California. She ended up moving to St. Louis early in the summer of 2005. I don't think that St. Louis was the particular draw. Instead, she was seeking change in her life. By the time she came to help at Woodland Meadows, I was seeking a change in my life as well.

We provided documentation to the city evidencing the insurance litigation and the millions held up by the bond trustee. City officials feigned understanding while they asked us for documentation on the tenants, trying to determine who lived where. This seemed unusual, but we went ahead and provided what was requested. In hindsight, the city was gathering data to plan the relocation of all of our tenants months before we even knew of a relocation. We were being cooperative, but city officials were planning to betray us.

JOHN GREGORY

In summer 2005, Franklin Capital, our tax credit investor, insisted that a management change was needed at Woodland Meadows. Franklin had purchased the Low Income Housing Tax Credits that had been awarded to Woodland Meadows. I was to receive a million dollars a year for eight years if I kept Woodland Meadows open, operating, in good condition, and well-occupied with low income tenants. Before the ice storm, these appeared easy to satisfy. However, these simple requirements were now appearing more and more challenging to comply with.

Franklin thought I needed help—professional help. Thus, they convinced me that we needed to bring in a new management company, jettison John Gregory as manager, and make some other personnel changes. By this point, John had expanded on the TEACH program started at Woodland Meadows by creating TEACH Staffing, a temporary staffing agency providing labor to local businesses. In addition, John started TEACH Tec, a non-profit training program to train workers. Although open to all, the TEACH entities continued to focus on the group often neglected by other programs: young African American males.

However, Flaherty & Collins, the new management company, did little to right Woodland Meadows' course, and instead charged higher management fees that sucked up some of our dwindling income. Flaherty & Collins did background checks on all our employees and the results were challenging. I did manage to lobby to keep several employees despite their felonious pasts. For those with the most nefarious pasts, Flaherty & Collins believed that the liability was too great. I felt terrible, as if Franklin and Flaherty & Collins were Child Protective Services, coming in to break up our family "for our own good." Some could stay, but others would go. This also made fixing Woodland Meadows even more difficult as our family weakened and ties were strained. Thankfully, John hired some of the fired felons and was able to get them work. Flaherty & Collins agreed to continue to allow TEACH Staffing to provide temporary employees, so we still maintained some contact despite the break up. Still, my foundation was crumbling.

By September 2005, Flaherty & Collins felt overwhelmed and abruptly resigned. No other management company wanted to get involved, so Woodland Meadows became self-managed by the remaining staff and me. In retrospect, Franklin and Flaherty & Collins came in, tore up the family, made our mess even worse, and then slinked away. Now that everyone had been scattered, I could not recreate the team. Besides, I was having trouble paying the scaled-down squad I had left.

Sadly, John Gregory ran into some challenges in later years. Cash flow must have been tight because TEACH Tec reportedly did not make their entire required payroll tax payments to the IRS from 2007 to 2010. In addition, he allegedly assisted a local nightclub owner and former Woodland Meadows contractor, Kevin Hightower, by converting his father's trust funds to personal use, instead of charitable purposes. Additionally, John was accused of falsifying records to mask these misdeeds. John was a great friend and ally, and I was saddened to hear that in December 2013 he was sentenced to one year and one day in jail. This man who worked so tirelessly to keep others out of prison was now imprisoned himself.

SEVEN WORDS KILLED A DREAM

"We're going to shut down Woodland Meadows," said City of Columbus Deputy Director of Development Trudy Bartley. Those seven words killed a dream. I was meeting with several city officials along with Woodland Meadows' new property manager, Verria, in a conference room at the city's building department. This was a few weeks before Thanksgiving 2005 at what I had expected to be a routine weekly meeting with city officials to share our progress in the rebuilding of Woodland Meadows. The insurance claim had not been settled and we were still waiting on a resolution.

As we learned, insurance companies scour claims looking for deficiencies and errors which they can then use as excuses to not pay claims or at least delay payments as long as possible. The stress of non-payment builds to a boil and the insured eventually capitulates, agreeing to a reduced settlement. This is what the insurers want to happen, and whatever legal fees they spend are worthwhile as the longer they hold onto the claim money, the less you are likely to accept in settlement. Although I would later use these same tactics to settle my unaffordable debts, here this powerful scheme was being utilized to great effect against me. This was my first exposure to the potency of these maneuvers.

"We're going to shut down Woodland Meadows." Trudy delivered these words matter-of-factly, as if she were sharing an obligatory "good morning" with a co-worker she dislikes, but feels bound to make nice to. The city was alleging the prior owner, P.M. Group, had left a beam in the basement of each building unreinforced. According to the city, this construction shortcut rendered the buildings subject to "imminent collapse." However, we had commissioned engineering studies, which determined that the buildings were safe and not structurally compromised. Even more frustrating to me, we pulled copies of city inspection records showing that, when P.M. Group's contractors erected these beams, city inspectors had inspected and signed off that the work was satisfactory.

We had been transparent and cooperative, realizing that this was an imperfect situation for all, and naively expected the same treatment in return. We had willingly opened our doors to all of their requested inspections and now they were turning on us, grasping for justification to tear us down. I felt unjustly attacked.

"We're going to shut down Woodland Meadows." I had trouble responding. I take after my mother, who avoids conflict and is always the peacemaker. This has generally served me well in life, as I often view both perspectives in a confrontation and broker even-handed compromises. However, as my heartbeat sped up and my cheeks flushed, I could not stand up and confront this steamroller daring me with engine revs. In fact, I felt suffocated. All the months of uncertainty and scrambling to rebuild caught up with me and I suddenly felt exhausted. Still, I could not give up, as the closing of Woodland Meadows would trigger an unfathomable burn zone with creditors. I could taste bile as my liver backwashed.

"Okay," I eked out. I was surrounded by city officials and this was the only response I could muster to respond to a death sentence determined by false evidence: the construction short-cut was over eight years old and no building had shown any evidence of potential collapse. As I spoke, I immediately felt that I let myself down and knew that I would look back on this moment with a plethora of more potent responses. But the opportunity had passed. I should have been furious. Instead, I was stoic.

"We want to set up a relocation center at the property," Trudy continued. For months now, Trudy had been helpful, offering and delivering on city assistance when she could. Closing the property had never been discussed before. The delays had extended longer than anyone had anticipated and I was financially fraying, although I kept my happy face on and tried to hide the extent of my fiscal vulnerability.

As I sat there, dumbfounded and envisioning sudden financial death, my debts started twisting around my brain. I sensed betrayal, as I had spent these millions with the city's knowledge of my predicament. Then, at my weakest moment, the city appeared to be forsaking me. I should have responded with outrage, but my shoulders tensed as the noose tightened.

"We will be bringing a team to Woodland Meadows to begin the relocation process and will need to use some of your offices," advised Trudy.

"Okay," was all I could muster.

"I'm sorry," Trudy said as we shook hands after the meeting. For a moment, Trudy looked like a Catholic nun who had just rapped my knuckles so hard that they bled. She was now trying to console me.

I was stunned, yet internally I was searching for a solution. I realized that Trudy was just the messenger and that others had written her script. A confrontation here would have yielded nothing, and could maybe even have made Trudy's blows easier for her to land.

Trudy must have realized that every word out of her mouth at the meeting was inconsistent with her prior representations, and to inflict these wounds on another had to upset some internal moral compass. Still, if her compass was askew, she did not show it. Meanwhile, my sails had gotten twisted as I had let the city's "help" guide me further into rock-riddled waters.

TEMPORARY RESTRAINING ORDERS

After the meeting, Verria and I drove back to Woodland Meadows in silence. I turned on the radio and heard a familiar tune. *"But I know there'll be some way, when I can swing everything back my way, like skyscrapers rising up, floor by floor."* This was my favorite Clash song. My mind started crafting a new plan.

That evening, I emailed my attorney to ask that he obtain Temporary Restraining Orders (TRO) to prevent the city from shutting down Woodland Meadows. I also capitulated and asked him to take whatever settlement deal the insurer offered next. Then, I emailed Trudy and advised that we would not cooperate with the city's relocation. Through all this, I recognized that the Angel of Death was gaining strength as I was losing mine.

"Woodland Meadows Owner to Fight Evacuation Orders" screamed the headline in the *Dispatch:*

> *"We've been told the buildings are subject to imminent collapse,' Newbery said yesterday. 'We dispute that.'... Newbery now says it was a mistake to cooperate with the city... 'I felt like a sucker, honestly,' he said. 'Our cooperation did not count for much... To facilitate the demise of the property on our own does not make sense.'"*

Entering a court fight with the city, I felt like "Tank Man," the nickname of the anonymous man who stood in front of a column of tanks on June 5, 1989, the morning after the Chinese military had suppressed the Tiananmen Square protests by force. The TRO hearing was in November 2005. On the eve of the hearing, the city appeared to concede that their case was feeble and lacking merit. Thus, they agreed to consent to the TRO provided I made consistent progress in the restoration.

The court did award me the TRO, preventing the trumped-up city-ordered evacuation, and required that we complete restoration with six months under the supervision of a court-ordered monitor. I was re-energized. I had survived the burn zone. I was relieved.

"The message here is: We can do it," I was quoted in the *Dispatch* on Dec. 6, 2005. "We're confident we can turn this around. We've had a number of setbacks that were a cause for concern. But we are still intent on making this a safe and quality home."

Within a few weeks, the monitor was reporting back to the

court that we were ahead of schedule. However, despite putting on a cooperative face at the TRO hearing, the city immediately asked HUD to pull our Section 8 subsidy contracts. HUD's Lynn Zapp called me, sounding indignant at the city's request as we had kept HUD apprised of our struggles and progress. Further, HUD had completed a Real Estate Assessment Center (REAC) inspection in October, which gave Woodland Meadows a passing grade and praised our significant strides in rebuilding from the ice storm.

After a December 1st "secret meeting" between HUD and the city, Lynn must have been swayed to the city's side. I heard from multiple sources that the meeting occurred. However, when we later filed a Freedom of Information Act request to get documents from the meeting, we were told that everything was verbal and no one took notes. This sounded implausible. Within days after the meeting, HUD gave us 30 days to complete the work that the court had given six months to complete—an impossible request.

In an effort to get everyone on the same timeline, Judge Harland Hale asked HUD to attend a court hearing, but HUD refused, stating that, as a federal agency, they were not bound by a municipal court. HUD then joined forces with the city to issue vouchers to relocate the tenants. I started to taste bile regularly.

STAY POSITIVE & UPBEAT
"Stay Positive and Upbeat"—I wrote these four words at the top of my yellow "to-do" pad every day as I neared financial collapse.

Perhaps I was delusional, but this helped. I was never one to give up early, although this time I probably gave up too late.

I kept thinking that I could turn this ever-more-dire situation around, coming up with a plethora of ideas and cures for the fatal contagion that had inflicted Woodland Meadows. Looking back, I was like a desperate dad who pulled his young drowned child out of the backyard pool and kept performing CPR long after the child's soul had slipped away. Giving my best and seeing a project to the end had historically resulted in a positive outcome, but not this time.

Woodland Meadows was my pride. In 2003 and 2004, in the midst of the transformation, the whole property was teeming with positive activity. I remember my morning jogs, which ended with a route through the complex. When I stepped off of Gould Road and entered the complex through the parking lot on Chesterfield, I would feel a rush of adrenaline and joy. The red brick buildings were cleaned up and sparkling, and the neatly trimmed green grass shimmered in the shade of stately trees that were much older than any of the 1950s era buildings.

If only these sapient aged trees could have talked like Tolkien's Ents, they would surely speak the truth of the present and share tales of decades past. Their chronicles would have certainly included much pain borne by residents through the years as they struggled to thrive as members of America's underclass. I always feel a kinship with those who are abused or beaten down. I don't know why I do this and sometimes I wish I didn't. Maybe this is why I always hung out with the less popular kids, the outcasts, and have always tried to help up those pounded down by life. Woodland Meadows had been beaten down, but I had breathed life back into the complex and my efforts had flourished. I was proud of what I had accomplished. As I ran through the complex, I exchanged waves and pleasantries with many of the workers and tenants. These were the good times.

Now, Woodland Meadows was doomed. But I could not just let it slip away. It hurt to be there, to walk the now-emptying grounds, which had lost the sparkle and vitality of just months before. Units were now boarded up; moving vans were backed up to remove the lifeblood from the buildings. The seven-word death knell had started, with aluminum and other metal being removed as scrap. I authorized some of the recycling as this generated some sorely needed cash. However, soon many outsiders were grabbing what they could and the police ignored my requests for help. I felt devastated, like I did when I had to climb into the team van after abandoning my Tour of Mexico quest. At times, I felt like nothing was going to get better. Then I would write down "Stay Positive and Upbeat" on my trusty pad, and it seemed like maybe today would not be so bad, that maybe some experimental surgery could bring my kid back to life.

I don't cry often—men aren't supposed to do so, at least in public. Historically, I would run to calm my mind and revel in the endorphins that followed. However, running wasn't quite as fun anymore and now seemed like a chore. I ate more, ran less, and gained some weight. I even went to Macy's and bought some pants with an expandable waistline to accommodate my spreading girth. These were my "fat pants." I wore them often during this period of strife.

To escape, I would cook popcorn in a hot air popper and binge on DVD's late at night in my apartment above the office at Woodland Meadows. My favorite was *"Bend It Like Beckham,"* the story of Jess, a teenage Indian girl in England. She was a fantastic soccer player, but was stymied in her pursuit by family and cultural traditions.

At a low point, like I was feeling then, Jess asks her coach "Why are you doing this to me, Joe? Every time I talk myself out of it, you come around and make it sound so easy."

Coach Joe replied, "I guess I don't want to give up on you."

At Woodland Meadows, I didn't want to give up on myself. Despite enormous obstacles, in the end Jess' family supports her, she scores the winning goal in the championship, and earns a soccer scholarship to an American college. Her future was now happy. Maybe that could happen to me? I must have watched the movie over 50 times in my final year at Woodland Meadows. The familiarity and happy ending reinforced in my mind a fantasy where I could bend it like Beckham and everything would return to happier times.

As the pall of death started to shroud over the complex, I became numb and emotionless. This burn zone appeared to have no end. As tenant families departed, creditors arrived, demanding money. The world seemed darker than before. Woodland Meadows will be stuck in my head until I die. I can still see the smiles from when I ran through the complex, the laughter at the TEACH class, the former felons who were now company owners and full of youthful optimism. Yet, my wide-eyed confidence died. I now step more carefully in life and particularly business, realizing that failure always lurks nearby. I still have a lot to contribute to the world, and I can still be optimistic, but my idealism perished in 2006 and is buried within Woodland Meadows.

At this point, I had a choice. I could either feel bad for myself, which I did sometimes, or I could rummage through my mind to find a means to turn this devilish experience into a positive. I so wanted the latter. I needed a new map for life.

ANTI-BLACK RACISM

"If there's one thing missing in our country, it's an acknowledgment of the broad humanity of black folks. Racism—and anti-black racism in particular—is the belief that there's something wrong with black people."

— TA-NEHISI COATES

I owe my existence to black people. You see, my mum was engaged to another man, Michael Dabbs, before my father. "If a black man walked into a bar, I'd walk out," said Dabbs in 1949. My mum was mortified upon hearing these words. Shortly thereafter, she called off the engagement. Luckily, many years later, she met my father. If it weren't for her principles, I wouldn't be here.

The majority of Woodland Meadows' residents, employees, and ex-felon workers were African American. My father is Argentine and my mother is British, which makes my skin a very light shade of Hispanic or a slightly dark shade of white, depending on one's perspective. My name is Jorge, but I don't speak Spanish. I go by "George," but I used to check "Hispanic" on loan applications. I am a minority business owner and my wife is African American.

At Christmas, we usually visit my wife's family first. Their Christmas dinner is the same as my family's dinner, and I suspect the same as most families' dinner: food, drink, conversation, presents, maybe a glimpse of a Lakers game on TV, and lots of love.

Most of the hundreds of ex-felons who worked at Woodland Meadows through TEACH were young African American males. If I walked past any of these guys in a dark alley, my heart would beat faster and my gait would quicken. The reaction is subconscious, the result of growing up in an America where the villains on TV and other media tend to be African American while whites are frequently portrayed with positive imagery. Many news outlets pander to the white majority and perpetuate the perspective that whites may commit crimes, but African Americans are criminals.

Describing the heart-wrenching agony as thousands of African Americans cried for help from rooftops, bridges, and anywhere else dry in New Orleans following Hurricane Katrina, the *African Independent* observed that the white majority's pain subsided once news was broadcast of African Americans looting stores for food, water, diapers, and baby formula:

> *"[The] Majority of White Americans who were heart broken by images of a Black third world at their doorstep coasts*

and neighborhoods could henceforth sleep at last with the customary belief that Blacks deserve what happens to them, as they are thugs and thieves, unrestrained looters..."

Fascinatingly, as media images of New Orleans' African American residents wading through hurricane-induced floodwaters with "looted" food were broadcast around the world, whites were described as having "found" food. The best excuse for mistreatment of African Americans is to blame African Americans.

Unarmed Rodney King got a healthy beating by five white police officers, *but he deserved it because he was on PCP* (untrue). Unarmed Michael Brown was killed by a white police officer, *but he deserved it because he was charging the officer in a menacing fashion* (dubious). Unarmed Oscar Grant got shot in the back and killed by a white transit police officer while he lay face down, *but he deserved it because he was resisting arrest* (untrue). Unarmed Eric Garner was killed by a white police officer, but, according to Congressman Peter King, *"If he had not had asthma, and a heart condition, and was so obese, he would not have died from this."* (Bullshit). Trayvon Martin was shot dead by a neighborhood watch patrolmen, but according to rocker and conservative radio show host Ted Nugent, *he "got justice" because he was a "17-year-old dope smoking, racist gangsta wannabe."* (Why do people listen to Ted Nugent?)

According to the FBI, between 2005 and 2012 in the United States, white police officers killed an average of two African Americans per week. This is almost like a national weekly quota: write a certain amount of speeding tickets, harass a certain number of minorities, and kill two African Americans. The actual count is likely much higher, as only 750 of the 17,000 law enforcement agencies in this country voluntarily report to the FBI's database.

The majority of these are treated as "justifiable homicides" because the victims are blamed for getting killed. In the United States, African Americans are typically assumed to be at fault, no matter how minor the offense. Even when African Americans clearly do well for the community, credit is often muted or even misappropriated by white people. Almost 500 African Americans and Hispanics perished in the 9/11 attacks, including firemen, bankers, security guards, and many others. However, 9/11 commemoratives and memorials have been largely devoid of minorities. LeRoy Wilson Homer Jr. was an African American pilot, husband and father flying United Flight 93, which was downed by terrorists. Yet when the critically acclaimed movie "United 93" was released in 2006, Homer was depicted by a white actor.

At Woodland Meadows, hundreds of African American men were busting media stereotypes and making a legal living, learning new skills, and contributing to their families and their community. The men involved perpetuated positive change, and other men facing comparable obstacles received similar opportunities. In the wake of Woodland Meadows's demise, the loss of its ongoing showcase for the success of these African American young men proved to be the ice storm's greatest calamity.

GETTING KICKED IN THE TEETH
Walt Disney once said that, "you may not realize it when it

happens, but a kick in the teeth may be the best thing in the world for you." I was kicked in the teeth over and over from 2005 to 2007, a beating that still marks me today. During these exceptionally challenging times, I was maligned, financially gutted, and publicly shamed. I survived, moved forward, and tried not to think about what happened.

A spokesman for the mayor's office told the *Dispatch* in December 2005 that unspecified criminal charges were being sought against me. My attorney called the city attorney's office and was advised that this was not true. Still, there was no retraction, no correction. Why? As the ex-felon TEACH workers likely experienced, authorities know when they have you down with their knee on your neck. Why apologize for a few extra baton blows or, in my case, self-serving slander?

Woodland Meadows got killed by authorities, *but I deserved it because I was a schemer* (per Columbus city attorney*), a slumlord* (per *The Columbus Dispatch*)*, public enemy #1* (per Mayor Michael Coleman*) and under criminal investigation* (all untrue).

WOODLAND MEADOWS OWNER ARRESTED

"You are in my custody now," said the police officer. I had just sat down at a conference table with representatives of the City of Beaumont, Texas' fire, building, health, and police departments in November 2006.

"What does that mean?" I inquired.

"There was an arrest warrant issued after you failed to appear," he replied. I knew this. The city had called me the week prior and advised me that they had sent me a notice to appear in court to answer criminal housing code violations at Pear Orchard Apartments in Beaumont.

I had acquired the 150-unit complex following Hurricane Rita, which hit in September 2005, and was assembling government financing to help fund a renovation. However, the process was taking a long time. The city had recently started getting tough on the owners of the many Hurricane-damaged properties that still needed repairs, including Pear Orchard. There was a clogged outside drain, which created standing water, and a large stump remained from a tree damaged in the storm.

"I understand that, but the notice was mailed to an old address," I shared, as the notice was mailed to 3312 Columbus Court, my old Woodland Meadows address. I had moved out four months prior when the property closed in June 2006. Besides, once the Beaumont official called, I had asked the manager to have the stump removed and clear the drain to address the standing water.

"Yes, but we just need to clear this up with the judge," he said. "A bench warrant was issued and the judge knows you are in town. He agreed to stay late."

I was here for a city council hearing, which included an update on the bond issue I had proposed to fund the renovation of Pear Orchard, which suffered severe hurricane damage.

"We can go after the city council meeting?" I asked.

"Yes, you can follow me over in your car," he replied.

After the council meeting, I tailed the officer to the courthouse. However, the judge had left. After some wrangling, the officer asked me to post $350 bail, which I charged on a credit card. I was never handcuffed, put in jail, or even read my Miranda rights. The charge was eventually resolved through deferred adjudication and my criminal record expunged.

This must have been a slow news day in Beaumont, however, because the next day the big news story locally was "Apartment Owner Arrested at City Council Hearing." In the short-term, there was no fallout. However, the window into the world provided by the Internet is not always helpful. Every piece of news, good or bad, lives forever. A couple of weeks later, I had a phone call.

"Tell me about your arrest in Beaumont," asked Mark Ferenchik of Columbus' *Dispatch*. Bile gurgled up my throat.

"Mark, the arrest was for failure to appear," I said, clenching my teeth. "It was nothing."

"Woodland Meadows Owner Arrested," screamed the *Dispatch* headline the next day. That evening, Mayor Michael Coleman appeared on all the news channels, stomping on my grave. He thought he had won.

$32 MILLION AND THE SPOILS OF WAR
The insurance claim from the Woodland Meadows disaster was

$32 million. If only I had closed Woodland Meadows promptly after the storm, I could have paid off our mortgage and investors, recouped my investment, demolished the buildings, and sold the vacant land to clear a nice gain. That would have been the easy route out and, in hindsight, certainly the one I should have taken. However, I never even considered this, as I was intent to make Woodland Meadows work.

Instead, I took the more challenging path, one riddled with flooded basements, lawsuits, and betrayal. My life would be forever changed. To rebuild seemed noble and proper in order to perpetuate the community, which was operated by and for the residents. We wanted to prove the long-term viability of a new ideal, a model in which large-scale low-income housing projects could flourish and become self-supporting assets to their communities. The storm disrupted our mission, but I was intent to show that this was merely an interruption.

Where did $32 million go? $18 million in mitigation costs, $13.5 million to settle the mortgage, $8 million squandered on restoration costs for buildings eventually vacated and demolished, and $4 million for operating costs attributed to Loss of Rents, which were rents lost as we allowed many tenants to not pay their rent for periods while their units were restored, along with allowing other families to break their leases and move.

This partial list totals $43.5 million. Add legal fees, interest, and loan fees on money borrowed on other properties to keep Woodland Meadows going and we got close to $50 million. Thus, the $32 million was gone and still left millions in unpaid creditors and my multi-million dollar pre-storm investment wiped out. This all happened in slow motion, with me going from the top of the world in December 2004 to financially flat-lining 18 months later.

During this period, I never stepped back and took a global assessment to make proactive decisions. Instead, I made decisions in a reactionary mode, akin to those on a battlefield. This was not ideal and I did not always make the best choices, ceding ground to the enemy.

In early 2006, as the relocation proceeded, the city was clear that they would not support the continued use of my property as affordable housing. Instead, the city dangled grants and favorable financing in front of me. These could be mine if I redeveloped the site as a mixed-use property, maybe senior housing, some higher end homes, and commercial buildings. This dissuaded me from filing a lawsuit against the city and seemed like a reasonable compromise. The city asked that I bring in other partners, and even introduced several large city-favored groups to participate. I felt that this was an equitable resolution and maybe I could emerge okay from this tribulation.

I spent precious dollars on redevelopment plans and studies, allowed the city to move the relocation offices to Woodland Meadows' administration building, and even permitted city police and fire departments to use the vacant buildings for training. Police were honing their tactical skills while the fire department set building fires and then doused them as part of exercises. The expectation was that the buildings would be demolished, so that this was a positive interim use.

This all seemed fair to me—reciprocal. I met regularly with city officials and my new redevelopment partners. However, their goal was to ensure that I cooperated with the relocation so they could get every tenant out. As soon as the final tenant vacated Woodland Meadows, city officials stopped returning my calls.

"Newbery is a man of integrity. Maybe he has an expectation that people would deal with him the same way, and I think he got a dose of maybe not so much. People are pretty rotten out there," observed former Woodland Meadows resident Draga Sikanovski in a 2014 interview. The city passed along word that they would not support a redevelopment in which I was involved. I had been betrayed again. I had scratched the city's back, but they were gouging at my eyes. In the end, I lost and the city of Columbus took Woodland Meadows as the spoils of this war. However, before my fate was sealed, I had to write the hardest letter of my life.

Dec. 6, 2006

Dear Mayor Coleman,

"Woodland Meadows is cleaner, safer, and better managed in the 10 months since Newbery bought it. There's been a 38.7% decrease in crime. We think Mr. Newbery has made great improvements." —Bruce Miller, president of North Harding Road Block Watch in November 2003 Columbus Dispatch article.

"Many people did not feel how a low-income neighborhood besieged by drugs and gang violence could turn itself around.

But I have seen it with my own eyes: thanks to you, Woodland Meadows is a changed community. The changes occurring at Woodland Meadows are impressive! I commend you for providing employment to over 200 African American men. The renovation efforts represent a community where jobs are created, families have safe, decent, and affordable housing, and lives are better. Woodland Meadows represents hope. Winning efforts such as yours are what makes the city of Columbus and state of Ohio one of the best places to live."
—State Representative Larry Price in February 2004 letter.

"There exists a gathering storm that could represent the largest concentration of privately-owned vacant and abandoned buildings in our city's history. I am speaking of Woodland Meadows, the future of this Eastside complex is in doubt. I am here to say to the current owner and any future owner of the property that we are willing to work with you to turn this property into an asset" —you in February 2006 State of City address."

When I read your State of the City address, I was warmed by your words. You see, I have been renovating properties for 12 years, starting with a fourplex in South Central Los Angeles in 1992 and progressively building up to larger and more challenging buildings. By the time I purchased Woodland Meadows on the last day of 2002, I had successfully renovated hundreds of buildings and had amassed an impressive track record.

My confidence was strong, as I had taken on problem housing where everyone else had failed and became the one who finally got it right: to wit, in 1998, when I bought the 298-unit Ford Hotel on Los Angeles' Skid Row, the four prior owners had all gone to jail for slum violations at the property. Of course, no one else wanted to buy it as it represented a sure ticket to jail, so I bought the Ford at a great discount and was able to finally be the one to satisfy the city and clear all the violations.

Thus, when I bought Woodland Meadows, I believed that my formula of being hands-on, employing the community as part of the turnaround, and good old-fashioned hard work would succeed. Remember, I moved into an apartment at Woodland Meadows just above the office and was there to witness the problems first-hand and solve situations first-hand. This work paid off, as crime plummeted at the complex and in the surrounding neighborhoods, physical conditions improved drastically, and occupancy and collections soared. I even generated some rare positive press for Woodland Meadows in the local media.

Not everything was perfect, though. The costs of the renovations exceeded my projections, and the property was so big that by the time we had renovated all 122-buildings, it seemed unanticipated new problems kept popping up. For instance, the city sewer system on our part of the Eastside had not yet been enlarged, so our basement units (as well as the basements of nearby homeowners) fell victim to backups during heavy rains, which was certainly not something I had expected. Although the property's financial performance had improved significantly and we had seven-figure reserves, the additional cash needs required that I infuse significant *personal cash into the project, as well as borrow heavily. In the end, this kind of felt like when you are at a blackjack table and you end up putting all your chips on one bet, and in this case, my bet was on Woodland Meadows.*

Nevertheless, income was increasing, we succeeded in obtaining the bond issue to replace our higher-rate construction financing, and we syndicated our tax credits, which were to provide me over a million a year for eight years provided the property was maintained as affordable housing. This million a year was to go towards repaying the money I had borrowed as well as my personal capital, and the property's cash flow would represent my earnings.

When the ice storm occurred in December 2004, I was confronted with a situation unlike any I had ever faced before. We allowed tenants to break leases and move off the property, but hundreds of families stayed. I gave my credit card out to buy temporary heaters, rent dozens of hotel rooms, and try to accommodate the displaced families.

You and the city also came to the aid of the hundreds of families who likewise were confronted with an extraordinary situation. In retrospect, I should have made the decision to close the complex then until the buildings could be restored. Even if I did, though, where would all the hundreds of remaining families go in the middle of winter? Also, my million a year from the tax credit syndicator was to be paid only if I reached and maintained 80% occupancy, and we had just reached that figure shortly before the storm. So, financial reality dictated that Woodland Meadows be restored as promptly as possible. Besides, we were sufficiently insured.

We contracted with Belfor, an international disaster remediation contractor, and truckloads of equipment and armies of workers soon arrived at Woodland Meadows. Rows of generators, temporary heaters, and drying equipment hummed 24/7 as we tried to make the conditions as good as possible. We pulled out all the damaged drywall to prevent the spread of mold, and started a conversion to electric heat to replace the cracked boilers, amongst hundreds of other restoration improvements.

I think even Belfor underestimated the magnitude of the damage, and the insurer certainly had great challenges assessing all the wounds that had been inflicted on Woodland Meadows. Finally, the claim well exceeded the insurer's $5,000,000 threshold, resulting in reinsurance kicking in. This represented great delays in paying the claim, which spooked Belfor and our bondholders Allstate, who got skittish and held back the insurance funds. When Allstate held the funds, Belfor abandoned the project and I scrambled to try to keep all the pieces together. About the same time, your building inspectors increased their inspections and discovered some structural shortcuts by former owners PM Group, which only became evident because we had removed all the drywall in the basement units. Soon, even though I was meeting weekly with Trudy Bartley, Dana Rose, and others on your team, the three-day evacuation orders were issued.

By this time, my head was spinning, income was shrinking, my reserves were drained, and everyone was looking to me to solve what was spiraling into an impossible predicament. I am always one to try to work things out amicably, but I had to go to court to get those Temporary Restraining Orders if I had any hope of salvaging what by this point had become everything I had earned over the prior 12 years. I apologize if you felt that this action was disharmonious, but I could not let Woodland Meadows be vacated and be financially wiped out.

When we reached the Settlement Agreement, our investors felt somewhat reassured, and we were able to fund and make significant progress towards addressing the city's concerns. However, then HUD *terminated our contract, and the impossible predicament became even more unimaginable. My investors started cutting me off, all the money I had borrowed on my other properties for the benefit of Woodland Meadows came due, and 2006 has sunk into a crushing year.*

Nevertheless, I have kept my head up and somehow have managed to stay operational as a developer, although I have almost no staff anymore. I tried to take you up on your State of the City offer, and retained Matt Kallner and John Kennedy, both well-credentialed attorneys with good city track records, to help facilitate a redevelopment plan. We had several meetings with Mark Barbash, Trudy Bartley, Boyce Safford, representatives of the Ohio Housing Finance Agency, and others in a quest to find the ideal redevelopment plan. Your team advised me to be cooperative with the relocation, and I did so, going as far as moving the relocation office into the Woodland Meadows Leasing Office.

Your team wanted rent rolls and reports on existing tenants, and we provided these. Your team suggested that support would be easier if I obtained partners and other participants in the project, and I brought in Columbus Housing Partners, Gorsuch Management, Rockford Homes, Beacon Management, Kimco Development, Atlantic Coast Developers, Eddie George's EDGE Group, and Meacham Appel Architects. Your team recommended that a mixed-use project would be received most favorably, and we crafted a plan with single-family homes, both rental and for sale, elderly housing, and commercial. Your team suggested possible financing tools from the city and others, and we incorporated these into our proformas. Your team suggested that I get community support, so we met with community leaders and our neighbors, and received their input and generated a number of calls to your offices in support of our redevelopment plans. Your team wanted me to meet with your planning department, and we did this. Your team wanted detailed financial projections, and these were provided.

By June, we had furnished everything your team had requested, including copies of signed purchase offers from a bevy of top-quality partners and participants. In addition, I had regular meetings with your code enforcement, building, and city attorney staff, and responded to all of their requests, and maintained the property as best I could. We allowed your fire department and police department, as well as all

Central Ohio law enforcement and fire agencies, to use the vacant Woodland Meadows for training.

Thus, I believe that I have demonstrated a willingness to work with the city to craft the best possible redevelopment of Woodland Meadows. Likewise, true to the words in your State of the City address, the city demonstrated your willingness to work with me. However, sometime after the last meeting in late June, your team stopped responding and I heard feedback that the city would not support a redevelopment plan in which I was involved. This was a bit shocking, as I had expended precious resources on architects and land use planners as we all appeared to have been making great progress. Oddly, all the momentum we were collectively generating seemed to terminate about the same time the last tenant moved out of Woodland Meadows.

This brings us to the present. I have written this letter to give you some background and answer the question many people ask of me: why don't you just walk away from Woodland Meadows? I hope you see now that I can't, as this represents everything I have. My personal future is tied to the fate of Woodland Meadows. Thus, I will continue to fight if I have to. However, I believe that we both have the same goal, which is to "turn this property into an asset."

Thus, I propose that we meet and try to take steps towards this common goal. I am available at your convenience— please contact me.

Jorge Newbery

Managing Member, Woodland Meadows Partners LLC

Mayor Coleman never responded. Instead, a few weeks later in a January 2007 interview with *Call & Post,* the mayor proclaimed that he had "declared war" against me.

In 2010, long after Woodland Meadows had been reduced to the largest vacant lot in the city of Columbus, I attended a real estate investor conference. There, a gentleman approached me as he recognized me as the former Woodland Meadows owner. He went on to describe an improbable scenario.

Back in 2002, he had attended the auction where I acquired Woodland Meadows. There, he was within earshot of another bidder who was there with city officials. After I had won, the city officials stood up to leave. Before departing, they shared a few words with the city-friendly bidder: "We will get it in time."

At that moment, like the flashback sequence at the end of a M. Night Shayamalan movie, everything seemed to make sense. Was I a pawn in a city game from the day I won the auction? Did the city, the *Dispatch,* and others collude to start hitting me with bad press even before the storm in order to derail me? Did the storm present an opportunity that they then seized upon, feigning help post storm, then pummeling me as I weakened until I was forced to relinquish my property? Woodland Meadows ended up in the city's hands and they still own it to this day.

CHAPTER FIVE

No One Wants to Work with a Loser

STRUGGLING THROUGH MY WOODLAND MEADOWS DOWN-
fall, I was an enamel loser. The uncertainty made me grind my
teeth at night. I had food and a place to stay. I had a car and a
cell phone and decent clothes. I had what I needed. In fact, my
Spartan life when I was broke was not that much different from
the Spartan life I led when I had millions of dollars in the bank.
Today was okay. Tomorrow made me nervous.

As soon as I got up in the morning, the first thing on my mind
was not family, friends, or dreams. Before brushing my teeth,
I went online to view my bank accounts and see what checks
had cleared the night before and whether my accounts had
slipped into the red. If overdrawn, then I needed to come up
with some cash and get it to the bank to plead with the bank
manager to pay the checks by 11:00 AM, before the prior day's
checks overdrew my account. All my accounts were struggling—
personal and business.

Ideally, I wouldn't have written the checks in the first place. But when there is a red notice and the gas is about to be shut off and *some* money was expected to come from somewhere soon, the best option at the time appeared to be to write the check and hope for the best. The same rule applied to my personal needs: if a credit card was due, I would mail it at the last possible moment and even slightly tear the bottom of the check in the middle of the routing number, as I heard that sometimes delayed processing.

Yes, $35 for each overdraft was bad, but bounced checks triggered even more fees from whomever I gave the check to. It felt like an accomplishment just to survive each day. Gone were the days when my creativity was utilized to improve my life and the lives of those around me. Instead, my mind was busy applying my ingenuity to keep my immense debt load from decimating me. I was paying for dreams past and could not afford new ones.

I had become enslaved to my creditors. I would make a payment here and one there—everything was behind, but I would pay any money I got my hands on to try to put out fires, buy time, and try to keep creditors at bay. I borrowed from friends and family in order to pay creditors. I sold everything: my buildings and even the used refrigerators and tools from Woodland Meadows, which I sold in bulk to other local apartment owners. This all went to pay creditors. Still, it was never enough and I was simply digging myself a deeper grave. This was no way to live.

I was 39 in 2005 when my life started to unravel. Today, if I could talk to my 39-year-old self, I would advise the following:

1. Once you recognized you were in over your head, stop paying EVERYONE. I kept hoping for a miracle. I was searching for a magic bullet and paying what I could, all of which I regret. In the end, I just delayed a financial death, which became inevitable.
2. Do not borrow from friends and family. In the end, creditors such as Bank of America will not take your lack of repayment personally. However, not repaying friends or family members can scar relationships for the rest of your life.
3. Do not sell everything—keep what you have.

I was ashamed. I was someone who my family and friends admired, who business associates and employees looked up to. People asked, "What happened to Jorge?" as though I got sick. One of my creditors even called my sister Charlene in Los Angeles speculating that I must have gotten hooked on drugs. Apparently, they were unaware of my straight edge lifestyle.

I tried to spare my parents from news of my collapse. Still, many years later, my father shared that he knew something had gone wrong. I took every call, every rumor, as a sign of my failure. I had always been a success, but now I had failed.

I considered filing for bankruptcy to put all this behind me. I remember going to see a bankruptcy attorney. I gathered all the documents necessary and completed all the paperwork. However, as I drove to the attorney's office to sign the final documents, my head was throbbing and I felt nauseous. I pulled over to the side of the road and turned onto a residential street. I parked and sat back. Just then, a car delivering newspapers drove by. I thought back to when I was seven and a paperboy, when I earned my first dollar. Now, more than three decades later, I had lost everything earned since that dollar. I had nothing to show for all my years of hard work, late nights, and sacrifice.

I felt like I was about to throw up. I opened my car door and put my head out of the car. I wanted to vomit, hoping that would make me feel better. But I just dry heaved a few times and the pain remained. An older lady walked by.

"Is everything okay?" she asked.

"Yes, everything is alright," I said, trying to sound as collected as possible. "I think I may have a touch of something."

"The flu is going around," she said in a maternal manner. "Drinking plenty of fluids usually helps."

"Something *is* going around," I said weakly, knowing that 'something' was unaffordable debt and not the flu.

"I hope you feel better," she said, walking away. "Have a good day."

"Yes, you too," I said. I retched one more time, loudly, and she looked back. I gave her a wave, as if to say *yep, still okay*. She kept walking.

I couldn't go through with filing the bankruptcy. It would mean admitting failure and I was too proud. The idea was too devastating in my mind. I could have been rid of millions and millions of dollars in debt. Still, I was repulsed and just couldn't do it. I called the attorney and left a voicemail that I wasn't going to proceed with the filing. I reasoned that I could make the money back and having bankruptcy on my record wouldn't help. Let the creditors keep coming at me; I could fend them off.

Now, when I go to the dentist, I am often asked if I smoke or drink coffee as they try to figure out what happened to my teeth. I don't smoke or drink, but the stress and uncertainty of this period of my life not only wore down my teeth and gums, it wore me down. I often awoke at night with my teeth clenched together like a vise, grinding away. My pearly whites had become pitted yellows. If I had known back then what to expect, my path would have been a lot easier. And I would not have been an enamel loser.

EVERYTHING IS OKAY

"Jorgie, is everything okay?" my dad asked. I was home for my father's 86th Birthday on July 14, 2006.

"Yes," I said. I had finally given up on correcting his pronunciation of my name. "Everything is okay." In reality, I felt shattered. I had not felt this way since after my defeat at the Tour of Mexico in 1988, when I started starving myself, and my mum and my sister took to calling me "Skull" due to my emaciation.

"Are you sure?" he prodded. I hadn't been home since Christmas as I was struggling and searching for the lessons in my defeat, just like I had in 1988. As I reflected, I realized that the Woodland Meadows episode was part political theater; part bad luck; part opportunistic thuggery by what I perceive as otherwise good people; part my excessive risk-taking; and part my fault particularly resulting from my overly optimistic "everything will work out" attitude as a serial entrepreneur. I knew that the only way to give myself a chance at massive gains was to expose myself to massive losses. I had lost.

"Yes, Dad. Everything is okay. Happy birthday," I said.

I was lying. What I should have said is: "Dad, everything's not okay. *I'm not okay.* Woodland Meadows is going to be demolished. I am losing everything that I built up over the last 17 years. I am in tens of millions of dollars in debt. I am even squandering enamel as I grind my teeth every night."

My dad and I in 2006

"That's okay, Jorgie," is how he would have likely replied. He would have hugged me. I would have started crying. I know this because I am tearing up as I write this, recollecting my father and the struggles we were both facing at the time. He had been diagnosed with stage 3 skin cancer more than a year earlier. His doctors gave him six months to live, and advised that he was untreatable due to his advanced age. His challenge was much greater than mine. He shared his dilemma with me, but I could not bring myself to share mine with him. Instead, I was bawling inside and did not want anyone else to see.

I wish I had been honest with him, though I'm sure he sensed at the time that I was holding back. "Everything will be okay," he would have assured me, as he held me close. I wish I had admitted my problems to my dad, my family, and myself. Perhaps this period of strife would have been easier. They would have supported me knowing what I was facing, and I would not have felt that I was battling by myself.

Looking back, the downfall of Woodland Meadows hardly seemed real. Although I had been brutally slandered by city officials, later rhetoric softened.

Columbus City Attorney Richard Pfeiffer told *Columbus C.E.O.* magazine in their July 2007 issue that:

> *"He [Newbery] has a business of going into distressed areas, using various government programs to either rebuild or rehabilitate things. We're not saying there was any wrongdoing here; we're saying there was a business plan that failed."*

This assessment made me feel a bit better, coming from a municipality which had previously labeled me a criminal, but that didn't help give me back all I had lost. Besides, I had a successful business plan aborted by the ice storm, and the city had done all they could to ensure that I failed.

I needed a new plan to succeed. I was broke with a crushing debt load. My credit was wrecked and the Woodland Meadows catastrophe was fresh. I could no longer be a real estate mogul. No one wanted to work with a loser.

The wise words of Nelson Mandela drifted through my mind like slow-moving clouds on a propitious spring day: "The greatest glory in living lies not in never failing, but in rising every time we fail." I was ravenous to rebuild myself, and wanted to take what I had learned and put my struggles and failures to productive use.

"Do you want some cake? It's your favorite: carrot," asked my dad, smiling.

"Yes, please," I said, cheering up. I did enjoy carrot cake. "I love you."

My father handed me a piece of carrot cake and a fork.

"*Everything is okay*," I thought to myself.

MR. NEWBERY
"Hey Mr. Newbery," said Emily Gomez by phone in August 2007.

She found some amusement in formally calling me Mr. Newbery despite a decade's long friendship.

"What's up, Emily?" I replied. Woodland Meadows was being demolished and I was living in a spare apartment at Country Woods Apartments, a 351-unit complex in Dayton, Ohio that I still owned, but which was in foreclosure. Emily was aware of the challenges I was experiencing.

"I need your help," she said. "My company closed down and I haven't found another job. The market is terrible. I am not making any money." Emily had been a loan officer ever since I met her. She was a divorced mother of three with a nice home in Glendale, Calif. The real estate market had hit a wall earlier in 2007 and her previously comfortable income had dried up.

"What can I do?" I asked.

"The bad news is that I have fallen behind on the house payments. The good news is that my lender said they would approve a short sale if I can find a buyer," she said. "Can you find an investor to buy my home and let me stay? I could pay lease payments and, when I get a new job, I could buy the home back."

"How much do you owe?" I asked.

"$600,000 plus the delinquent payments," she replied.

"How much will they accept?" I asked.

"$450,000," she said.

"Let me see what I can come up with," I advised. $150,000 is a significant discount, but this was simply a reflection of what the lender thought her home was worth at the time. I called a few investors to relay Emily's proposal. Most liked the concept, but believed that real estate prices were destined to fall further. Thus, they declined.

"Emily, I can't find anyone to help," I said. "I'm sorry."

"Thanks for trying, Mr. Newbery," she said.

I felt bad. I realized Emily's devastation was no different than mine. I had lost tens of millions of dollars and thousands of apartments. Emily was losing tens of thousands of dollars and a single home. Still, the hurt, humiliation, and frustration we felt were the same. Emily and I were close but, even so, revealing our inner torment was difficult. We both suffered alone.

On a long trail run in the ravine cutting through John Bryant Park, just east of Dayton in September 2007, my mind was reflecting, wandering, and searching. I had a vision: What if I created a company that could be a friend to all these millions of homeowners, like Emily, whose homes were suddenly worth much less than their mortgages? The company could purchase the homes on short sales and provide affordable leases and discounted repurchase options to the families.

Emily was foreclosed on. She was eventually evicted and her children moved in with their father. Emily put her stuff in storage and a friend allowed her to stay on her couch. As the mortgage business remained challenged, Emily took a job as a dog groomer, which paid her a fraction of what she previously earned.

"Is everything okay?" I asked her.

"Yes, everything's okay," she replied. Just as my father likely suspected all was not okay when he asked me the same question a year earlier, I realized that she was devastated inside, just like I was.

"Everything will work out," I said, trying to console her.

"Thanks, Mr. Newbery."

182 · BURN ZONES

CHAPTER SIX

American Homeowner Preservation

AFTER MY INSPIRING TRAIL RUN IN SEPTEMBER 2007, I emailed Jim Pietkiewicz, a municipal bond broker friend of mine, for his thoughts on my concept. Jim liked the idea, provided some feedback, and encouraged me to proceed, advising that his company Gardnyr Michael had interest in underwriting the bonds to fund my efforts. I started mapping out my new venture, American Homeowner Preservation, and my new life.

I was still living in my temporary apartment at Country Woods in Dayton. However, a foreclosure sale was looming and I needed to find a new place to live. My plan was to move to Cincinnati, which was searching for a solution to the foreclosure epidemic and indicated interest in supporting AHP.

I invited Verria, who was now my girlfriend, to once again move from St Louis, just as she had two years prior when she joined me in Columbus to become the last Woodland Meadows manager in history. A shared sense of loss had driven us together through my Woodland Meadows challenges: Verria had been very close to her mother, who was 43 when she lost her battle with cancer. The loss devastated Verria and she developed a debilitating illness which multiple doctors could not diagnose. It took years for her to get through and in the end no doctor could help her. She cured herself through a stringent diet and lifestyle changes. Even so, some of her health issues lingered.

"I'll come with you, but I am not going to live in the hood anymore," Verria said, referring to our surroundings at Woodland Meadows and Country Woods temporarily before she returned to St. Louis. "I get to pick where we live."

"That's fine, just be budget conscious," I said. I had brokered a few property sales and my commissions had funded my existence. We both looked on Craigslist for a new place to live—a fresh beginning.

We drove together to Cincinnati. I had found an apartment on Craigslist for $400 monthly. However, as we pulled up on a weekday morning, a group of young predominantly African American men clustered around the entrance.

"We are not living here," she said, eyeing the crowd.

"Come on, let's at least take a look," I said.

"No, I'm not," she said.

"It's $400," I said.

"I can see why," she said. "You agreed that I could choose."

"Okay," I relented. "Let's go see the highfalutin apartment you came up with." We drove to Hyde Park, the most expensive neighborhood in Cincinnati, where Verria had eyed an available apartment on Craigslist.

"This is it," she said. We pulled up to an older building on Madison Road, a busy street. I noticed a running shop about a mile away as we drove along Madison, and several runners here and there on the sidewalk. Between Pickwick, Woodland Meadows, and Country Woods, I had lived in affordable housing apartments for six years. I had forgotten what living in unaffordable neighborhoods felt like. After all I had been through, maybe I didn't feel that I deserved to live in an unaffordable neighborhood, at least not until I regained some financial strength.

"This is nice," I said, flatly, as we walked through the second-story two-bedroom unit. The building was older, but well-taken care of with spacious rooms and, to Verria's delight, a nice big kitchen with a pantry. "But what's this going to cost?"

"$800," she said.

"That's double the other place," I said. I have always been cheap, but at this point I really didn't have much money, so I had become almost miserly.

"You said I could pick," she said.

"What's the move-in cost?" I asked.

"$1,600," she said. "I have some saved. I can pay." I appreciated the offer, but it didn't feel right for Verria to pay for us to move into our new apartment.

"I have some," I said. We left a deposit.

"Now, let's find an office," Verria said. I had found one online for $500 monthly. As we drove up, there was a crowd grouped out front, similar to the entourage outside the $400 apartment earlier.

"We are not going in there," Verria said.

"We have an appointment," I said. "Let's go."

We got out and made our way through the boisterous crowd. As we got to the front, we saw the sign: Cincinnati Adult Parole Authority.

"That explains it," said Verria. "Let's go."

"No, let's see what the office looks like," I said, opening the office door for her to enter. "Besides, look at all the parole officers. This is probably a very safe building."

The $500 office was in the basement and even my optimistic eyes could not envision this as AHP headquarters. Besides, the suite smelled musty. I don't think anyone had actually worked down there in a long time. It was better suited for storage. We left and drove back down Reading Road towards the freeway.

"What about that building?" Verria asked, motioning towards what looked like a 12-story building with PNC Bank on the first floor.

"Looks expensive," I said.

"It can't be expensive," she said. "Not in this area. We're only a few blocks away from the $400 apartment we went to this morning."

"Get the number," I said, as I noticed the almost-vacant shopping center behind the building.

A few weeks later, we signed a $900 monthly lease on a nice new office in the PNC Bank Tower, which was built in the 1960s when the area was more prosperous. The building housed many state agencies and nonprofits, and was a well-maintained oasis in a rough-and-tumble area. I liked it.

In May 2008, American Homeowner Preservation opened for business. We hired two employees and I mostly brokered real estate to fund the fledgling operation. As the city of Columbus annihilated Woodland Meadows 100 miles away, I started rebuilding my life in Cincinnati.

NONPROFIT AHP

"Why do you want AHP to be nonprofit?" asked Verria, as I was in my office responding to an Internal Revenue Service documentation request, part of our effort to obtain tax-exempt status. I felt good being so close to turning my vision into reality.

"Because we can utilize municipal bonds to finance the homes that AHP will purchase from struggling families," I said. "And then provide the families with affordable leases and repurchase options to buy back their homes at discounted amounts."

"But how do you get the city or county or whoever to back the bonds?" she asked.

"The municipality reviews the deal, receives a fee, then issues the bonds," I said. "They don't back them."

"What's the difference?" she asked.

"Investors buy the bonds, and the money is used for the project," I said. "The revenue from the project, in this case from the leases, pays the bonds. This is just like Allstate buying the Woodland Meadows bonds issued by Franklin County. "

"Okay," she said, listening intently.

"If anything were to happen and the bonds were not paid, then the municipality is not responsible to pay the bonds," I said. "Bondholders can only look to the project as security. In AHP's case, the collateral is the homes."

"I kind of get it," she said.

"Look at it like this," I said. "The municipality is sort of like buying a laptop on eBay."

"Okay," she said, sounding intrigued

"eBay gets a small fee and most of the money goes to the laptop seller," I said. "The laptop is like the bonds."

"So, if I want to return the laptop, the money for the refund comes from the seller and not eBay?" she asked.

"Exactly," I said. "Same thing with bonds. The municipality is eBay, the conduit for the transaction."

NONPROFIT VS. NONPROFIT

In July 2008, the IRS issued a 501c3 designation memorializing AHP's nonprofit status. Initially, Cincinnati city officials indicated a willingness to support a bond issue to fund the program. Stephen Peterson of Allstate had indicated that he admired how I handled the Woodland Meadows crisis and liked the new AHP concept, so Allstate was the likely purchaser of these bonds. However, worried that upstart AHP may take funding away from existing housing programs, Legal Aid and the Catholic nuns at Working in Neighborhoods discredited AHP's unproven concept. They recommended that the city instead support their "tried and true," yet typically ineffective, foreclosure prevention programs.

Ironically, the Cincinnati Foreclosure Prevention Task Force, a coalition of these mostly impotent agencies, could not help Bonnie Tyler, one of the Task Force members whose home was in foreclosure. At risk of losing her family's home of over 18 years, Bonnie contacted AHP and asked if we could help. Despite all the other agencies that were part of the Task Force providing potential solutions, none of them were able to help. Bonnie advised us that she would take every document we asked her to sign to be reviewed by Legal Aid, which was fine with us. In the end, AHP succeeded and reduced her monthly payment from over $1,900 to $979 and provided her an option price to repurchase her home for $71,000, less than half the $145,000 she previously owed. In 2014, Bonnie repurchased her home at the discounted amount. One local nonprofit, the Cincinnati Homeownership Center, did appreciate the creativity of AHP's approach and proved an ally, inviting AHP to participate in their outreach events and referring many clients that they could not help.

AHP continued to search for other municipalities interested in issuing bonds to support AHP's mission. In September 2008, the Summit County Port Authority recognized the merit in AHP's plan and provided an inducement to issue $13,500,000 in tax-exempt bonds. The funds would be utilized to fund AHP's acquisition of homes in Summit County on short sales to allow the families to stay in the homes with affordable leases and options to repurchase their homes at significant discounts off their prior mortgage balances. By November, we were presenting the program to throngs of Summit County residents, who were eagerly signing up in an effort to save their homes. There was no cost to the homeowners and we planned to sell the Port Authority issued bonds to Allstate. Most importantly, there were no taxpayer dollars at risk.

However, in early January, some local housing nonprofits apparently grew errantly concerned that AHP would siphon off the dollars they would otherwise receive and banded together to rally against AHP's efforts. Echoing the Cincinnati arguments, they insisted that the concept was unproven and that the families would better be served by existing programs, which had showed little promise to date and in hindsight proved highly ineffective and a waste of taxpayer dollars. Despite these rumblings, the Port Authority continued to seem open to issuing the bonds, particularly as they earned a substantial fee to do so.

When AHP invited the *Akron Beacon Journal* to cover the story of a pilot short sale leaseback we completed in December 2008, they declined despite the fact that the family's monthly payment dropped by more than half and they could repurchase for less than a third of their prior balance. Instead, the *Journal* published an article broadcasting concerns that two of AHP's board members, including Emily, were in foreclosure themselves and that this was "concerning." In my mind, someone going through foreclosure is much better positioned to craft a tailored solution to foreclosure than someone who is financially flush. Experience *and then* devise—don't guess at what financial devastation must feel like. Hundreds of homeowners recognized the value in AHP's solution and voiced their support for us in emails and calls to the Port Authority. However, I could not escape my past.

"FUCK THA POLICE"

One evening in February 2009, Rick Armon, a reporter for the *Beacon Journal*, called me and left a chilling voicemail: "I want to ask you about the felony charges the Indianapolis Housing Police are planning to file against you." This was the first time I had heard of these allegations and I was stunned. My connection to Indianapolis was Keystone Towers, a 250-unit apartment complex, which I previously owned. However, Keystone had fallen into foreclosure and I was forced to sell as part of the Woodland Meadows' fallout. I called Mr. Armon back within an hour, but got no answer. I left a voicemail, but he did not call back.

Hearing "felony charges," my liver sprayed bile up my throat, a sensation I had not experienced since Woodland Meadows. I knew I hadn't done anything wrong, but jail is a whole different level of worry. I was still shaken from my Woodland Meadows burn zone and to be shell shocked so soon after was disconcerting—now I know what Post Traumatic Stress Disorder must feel like.

When I listened to Rick's voicemail, I was having dinner at a Cracker Barrel in Akron with AHP's Executive Director Rob Fredericks and Team Member Kimberly Reynolds, along with Verria. My mind was racing and they could tell I was distracted, so I shared the voicemail with them. They tried to console me with words like "Everything will be fine," and "I am sure you will get this straightened out." In my soul, I knew they were right. I probably would not go to jail if I hadn't done anything wrong, but then I thought of Ricky and the TEACH crews and how many times they said they were jailed when they didn't do anything wrong—and I believed them. Then I caught myself, "Wait. Don't worry. Calm down, you may be Hispanic, but you look white. False imprisonment only happens to African Americans in this country." This realization was both sickening and comforting. Nevertheless, I had been thrust into a burn zone. My teeth were in for some grinding that night.

The reporter's strategy of writing a hack job and then calling the target the evening before publication was reminiscent of Barbara Carmen of the *Dispatch*. The target has no time to refute the allegations. I see this over and over in news stories: "We were unable to reach the target for comment," and "phone messages for the target were not immediately returned." These both insinuate that maybe the target—in this case, me—is hiding.

"Fraud Alleged Against Housing Group's Backer" screamed the headline in the next morning's *Akron Beacon Journal*. The first line read, "Indianapolis Housing Police plan to seek felony fraud charges against a financial partner in American Homeowner Preservation." It sounded awfully dire. The Summit County Port Authority soon rescinded AHP's inducement in part due to these allegations. However, the Port Authority threw homeowners a bone and stated that they still liked AHP's plan and invited a local group to take up the mission. But no one did. The article continued to state that, "Telephone messages were left for Newbery," which was misleading, as only a single message was left. Further, no mention was made that the single message was left in the evening just hours before publication and that I had called back.

"Newbery and others allegedly accepted $55,487 in government money from 2005 to 2008, but then failed to fix up the vacant Keystone Towers, an apartment and retail complex in Indianapolis. They also owe nearly $800,000 in property taxes. Police will seek the charges through the Marion County prosecutor," continued the story. "Our position is that they've defrauded the government and they

*will be charged," Steve Golden, assistant police chief with
the Housing Police Department, said.*

I was stunned, as I had quitclaimed Keystone to another developer in 2006 at my lender's request. I called my attorney Wes Newhouse in Columbus and asked what to do. He contacted a criminal defense attorney, Sarah Riordan, in Indianapolis. I had to pay her a $5,000 retainer and she called Assistant Chief Golden to obtain a copy of the report, which had been sent to an old address and which I never received.

The report was in the form of a demand letter issued a few months prior to several parties: Keystone Towers, LLC (the entity I controlled, which previously owned the Indianapolis complex), the new owners, myself, and the mortgage holders on the property. The report was chock full of allegations; however, it was apparent that the police were unsure who was responsible for accepting the approximately $55,487 of Section 8 housing assistance payments during a period in which the complex allegedly did not meet housing quality standards, which they termed a "systematic, nationwide criminal conspiracy." Particularly perplexing was that, when I owned the complex, the Housing Authority was conducting inspections before families moved in and then annually during their tenancy. I wondered why the alleged housing deficiencies were not noted earlier, before the rent subsidies were paid. The report had requested reimbursement by late December 2008 in order to avoid criminal prosecution.

In May 2009, my attorney met with Officer Golden and provided documents evidencing that I did not own the complex during the period in question. After the meeting, she emailed me:

> I had a meeting with Steve Golden yesterday. I explained our position that you should not be on the hook for anything after the date on which you quitclaimed the property to your lender...He said his ultimate goal is to secure ownership of the property for the Housing Authority. If they can get Keystone Towers, it is possible that this case could go away.

"Fuck tha Police!"—the NWA song I heard blasted so many times in South Central—reverberated through my head. They knew I was innocent, but they were trying to create leverage by broadcasting the threat of felony criminal charges to the media in order to pressure me to relinquish a property I didn't even own. Ricky and the TEACH workers could surely relate.

My attorney advised me to relax, as the evidence was in my favor. In September 2009, I emailed my attorney:

> I would hope that if a reporter were to contact Mr. Golden again that he would be a bit more careful with his words, rather than essentially convicting me before the charges are even filed. Hopefully, your conversations have enlightened him to the fact that I have not had ties to Keystone Towers in a few years so that if he wants to create pressure to get someone to act on that building, then there are others he should be chasing.

No charges were ever filed. Nevertheless, news articles detailing these felony fraud allegations endure on the Internet. I was out the legal fees and some more tooth enamel. "Fuck tha Police!"

AHP BECOMES FOR-PROFIT

With bond financing off the table, AHP transitioned from a non-profit to a for-profit in 2009 and we offered the short sale leaseback opportunities to private investors. The model proved effective for investors and homeowners, but AHP's fee of $2,000 per transaction, paid by investors, barely supported our operation. Even though we were now for-profit, our finances still looked like a non-profit: we were barely scrapping by. I was determined that AHP would succeed, but financial realities dictated that we needed more volume: we had the demand from the homeowners as thousands were applying for AHP's help. However, the banks and servicers needed to approve the short sales, and this occurred on less than one in 10 submissions. In some particularly heinous cases, the lender would approve the short sale, but include a requirement that the seller family move out of their home, defeating AHP's mission.

In late 2010, Felix Salmon of Reuters recounted a typical AHP approval challenge:

> *I'm a longstanding fan of American Homeowner Preservation, which has found a clever way of keeping underwater homeowners in their homes while minimizing the loss to their lenders. Even the red-in-tooth-and-claw capitalists at Goldman Sachs can understand that. But not, it seems, the idiots at ING Direct.*

His article outlined ING's decision to no longer consider AHP short sales, moving us instead to their exclusionary list. All because AHP's strict policy to only work with investors who promised to keep sellers in their homes. Salmon continued:

This is vindictiveness, plain and simple. ING might get more money if it played ball with AHP, but the homeowner wouldn't suffer as much. Clearly, if ING is going to take "a significant loss," then it needs an element of suffering on the part of the borrower—it's a modern-day Shylock, demanding a pound of flesh which can do it no good whatsoever.

By the time Felix wrote this, AHP was exploring another direction: buying nonperforming mortgage debt from banks and lenders, instead of having homeowners initiate contact with AHP. The impediment to the AHP program was not the homeowners or the investors, but the lenders and servicers. I reasoned that if AHP could buy the loans, then we could do whatever we wanted with them. But how could we buy debt?

BUYING NONPERFORMING MORTGAGES AT BIG DISCOUNTS

You cannot just call Bank of America and offer to buy their defaulted mortgages. I reached out to some associates for input, but no one really knew. Then, by chance, I read an article in *Mortgage Daily* about Wealthbridge, a mortgage servicer that had just closed after a failed acquisition attempt by an investor group led by Joseph D'Urso, the former CEO of Wilshire Servicing, which had also recently closed. According to the article, Joe had lined up several large banks to transfer servicing of their nonperforming mortgages to Wealthbridge. I realized that I needed to connect with this guy! I found his profile on LinkedIn and messaged him:

"American Homeowner Preservation has an effective disposition strategy for nonperforming mortgages and would like to retain you to consult on how we can purchase pools of nonperforming mortgages. Please contact me."

Joe responded shortly thereafter to express his interest and we set up a call.

When Joe and I talked, he indicated that he liked AHP's concept and would be willing to make introductions. He asked for a fee of $4,000 to introduce me to eight mortgage sellers in one day. I flew to New York City and we met for breakfast. Joe was a smart, affable gentleman who had apparently developed strong relationships with many in the industry. We met with higher-ups at Bank of America and several large hedge funds, including Five Mile Capital.

By January 2011, AHP purchased a small pool of loans from Five Mile Capital, followed by a pool from Banco Popular in March. We learned by doing, figuring out due diligence and servicing of nonperforming loan pools as we went, just as I had with everything else in my life. We made a few mistakes, but the vision became reality. I learned that most buyers set their offers to buy nonperforming debt by assuming the worst possible outcome, which is foreclosing on the homeowner, which costs significant sums of time and money. If they could achieve a more expeditious solution, most debt buyers fare better.

AHP SUCCESS STORY

Here is a real life example: A gentleman in Maywood, a suburb of Chicago, had purchased his home in 2006 near the top of the market for over $200,000. He owed over $195,000 on the mortgage we purchased. Values had plummeted in this neighborhood, which is 82% African American, and the home is only worth $32,000 today. Nevertheless, the borrower paid his payments on time until 2010, when he was laid off from his 17-year job at Hinckley Springs Water. He fell behind on the mortgage payments, as he could not find a new job. However, in 2013, he had obtained an insurance license and was again employed. He applied for a modification through Ocwen, his servicer, but was denied.

AHP bought this loan for $9,600—30% of the current value of the home. When we contacted the borrower, he was skeptical as he thought our offer sounded "too good to be true." However, we convinced him that AHP had purchased his mortgage and he happily agreed to the modification we offered:

1. Payments reduced from $1,449 monthly to $320 monthly
2. $43,471 delinquency, representing several years of payments, was settled for $2,000
3. Principal was discounted from $195,418 to $29,600

Fantastically, our returns were better when we modified mortgages than if we foreclosed. Using strategies developed as a result of my Woodland Meadows' fiasco, AHP's borrower outreach and resolution efforts proved highly effective. By sharing some of the discounts we received from banks with the borrowers, we suddenly had a business that was viable, profitable, and scalable.

DO WELL & DO GOOD

The media had started taking note of AHP's pioneering strategies:

> *"American Homeowner Preservation is using private investor money to buy up mortgage pools and give the borrowers the solutions they need, not the ones that maximize profits for the company...It's an exciting development, and it shows you can do well and do good at the same time," said Dave Dayen of FDL.*

Martin Andelman of M1 Implode called AHP a "win-win operation."

Felix Salmon of Reuters wrote:

> *"...If you buy a mortgage and approach the homeowner with good will and a genuine desire to find a reasonable solution, it's amazing how often something mutually beneficial can be worked out. Indeed, a company called American Homeowner Preservation is doing just that: It's set up a hedge fund devoted to buying pools of defaulted mortgages and keeping homeowners in their homes, and it is making good money doing so. All it takes, really, is a little bit of compassion and an ability to be inventive."*

AHP's success can be directly attributed to the Woodland

Meadows' failure. During my period of strife, lessons were seared into my head on how to deal with overwhelming debt, armies of creditors, betrayal, humiliation, anger, and frustration. Millions of families in America are facing these same challenges today. As importantly, I learned how to persevere, recover, move on, and help these families who are trying to survive their own Woodland Meadows. I have suffered, and wanted to share my experiences to alleviate the suffering of others. This housing crisis is destined to displace more American families than any other disaster in history. The wreckage is immense, with families crushed, divorced, homeless, and/or staying in the basements and garages of friends and family. They are drained physically, mentally, and financially. It's a feeling I know all too well.

AHP EVOLUTION: NONPROFIT TO HEDGE FUND

I envisioned creating a hedge fund to facilitate larger investments, grow AHP, and help more families. Just like becoming a bike racer and even writing this book, I read everything I could on creating and running a hedge fund and started engaging attorneys, accountants, and other advisors in the mission. To connect with new investors, I realized that I would need to get out and spread the word about AHP, likely by speaking in front of large groups.

Despite shedding some of my shyness over the years, I was still uncomfortable presenting in front of sizeable audiences. This time, I wanted to share my passion. However, I thought if I just talked about AHP, then I would sound like a commercial. So I wrote something more personal, a speech I entitled "My Father's

Oasis of Tranquility" that I then presented at the Toastmasters club I had joined. I spoke about my father's Tai Chi practice, his dedication to leading a vibrant, tranquil life, and the influence that had on me. The speech was extraordinarily well received, and also reinforced a sense of tranquility within me as I recalled our runs and time together. Little by little, my anxiety fell away.

Toastmasters helped me prepare to launch AHP's hedge fund, and more support soon emerged. After Woodland Meadows collapsed, I stayed in touch with Stephen Peterson at Allstate. He appeared dismayed at what had transpired between the city and me at Woodland Meadows and was curious as to how I was recovering. Initially, he indicated Allstate's interest in acquiring the nonprofit AHP's bonds. Once that avenue closed due to the Port Authority's rescission, we would chat periodically as I shared AHP's challenges and successes. By mid-2011, Stephen had retired from Allstate and we talked more frequently, as he was then particularly intrigued by AHP's hedge fund prospects.

In August 2011, Stephen made a proposition: He would become a partner in AHP if we moved the operation to Chicago. He believed that we could raise significant capital, as the strategy was novel, and generated strong financial and social returns. Stephen was fond of saying that AHP was "a market solution to a social problem."

I sensed irony in the former overseer at Woodland Meadows' biggest creditor now going into business with a debtor that had spectacularly crashed and burned. Stephen had a front row seat to the Woodland Meadows debacle and, despite the city and *Dispatch* portraying me as a flop, Stephen witnessed the same show and interpreted my performance quite differently—and now even wanted to be my partner. This felt good to me, akin to when Alexi Grewal uttered those complimentary words to me in the Vulcan Tour over 20 years prior.

I thought that maybe connecting with Stephen was the reason that I had to go through my Woodland Meadows trials. Similar to after my Tour of Mexico debacle, I was searching to find a lesson and positive outcome in my failure. Even though I mostly remembered the many figurative tomatoes tossed at me and derisive boos I heard as I played through all the acts of Woodland Meadows, there were some—more than just Stephen—who applauded my performance. I needed to remember that.

CHAPTER SEVEN

Occupy Cincinnati

AS I MADE PLANS TO MOVE AHP FROM CINCINNATI TO CHI-
cago, I started hearing plans for Occupy Wall Street. In August
2011, Anonymous, an Internet activist group, released a video
announcing the Sep. 17th action. I was intrigued with the movement's message against social and economic inequality. On Sep.
25, I wrote a blog post called "Occupy Wall Street: Flashpoint of
an American Uprising," voicing my support of the movement
and encouraging others to involve themselves at local levels.

Hours after I posted "Flashpoint" to my blog on the now-defunct
ShameTheBanks.com website, I was loading the dishwasher
when I realized that I was encouraging others to start Occupy
movements in their own cities. Yet, there was no Occupy in Cincinnati where I lived. "*Why don't I start a local Occupy?*" I thought.

A few minutes later, I went on Facebook and created an Occupy
Cincinnati page. I then shared the page on the Occupy Wall

Street Facebook page. Within a few hours, the Occupy Cincinnati page had about 10 supporters. Within a few days, we crested 1,000 supporters and had rabid activity on the page 24/7. I started staying up until two or three every morning interacting with fellow Cincinnatians and others worldwide as we shared visions of utopia and inspiration at the progress of our Occupy Wall Street brethren in Zuccotti Park. True to the "no-leaders" ideal, I made everyone who was interested into a Facebook page moderator. We soon had dozens of moderators and an active Twitter feed. I felt like I had lit a match in a fireworks factory.

On Oct. 2, 2011, just a week later, we assembled at Sawyer Point to plan our Occupation. The meeting attracted a diverse group of over 100 supporters. I was awed by the speed with which we all came together. Some punks showed up in leather jackets and spiked hair. I thought back 30 years ago to my circle of punks, this loner's first real friends, as we shared ideas to build a better America. However, instead of improving over the last three decades, America's social and economic gaps had widened. That day in Cincinnati, we shared some of the same concepts to rebuild a broken country. I met Julie Ladd, a publicist whom I am still friends with today; Erik Crew, a social justice advocate for Ohio Justice & Policy Center; Sarah Burns, a high school student; Nathan Lane, an electrician; Carrie Pennington, a waitress at Olive Garden; Kristin Brand, an IT project manager; Aaron Roco, an organizer for the nonprofit Working America; Tim Brown, a writer; and many others, from teenagers to senior citizens. We soon divided up into committees: Legal, including several attorneys; Outreach/Publicity; Occupation; and others. A march was planned for the following Saturday, Oct. 8, 2011.

Within days, local news media was rife with Occupy Cincinnati coverage, we had over 10,000 supporters on Facebook, and people from all walks of life were offering support. In addition, there were many detractors, particularly as we lived in such a conservative bastion. Some singled me out, tweeting "Entrepreneur Jorge Newbery seems to be in the 1%, but is behind #OccupyCincinnati." They apparently were oblivious to my debt challenges.

By this time, images of police violently beating and pepper spraying Occupy supporters were coming out of New York. In many respects, the abuse generated more attention and more sympathy for Occupy. The Cincinnati police, fearful of replicating NYPD's challenges, reached out and wanted to meet the local Occupy organizers. A permit was issued for the march and rally in Fountain Square and the police wanted us to self-regulate troublemakers and appeared genuine in trying to ensure Saturday's events went peacefully. A proactive and respectful discourse between Occupy Cincinnati and the Cincinnati Police Department began.

The CPD's approach differed from the posture of the NYPD on Occupy Wall Street, the LAPD so many years before at the T.S.O.L. concert that precipitated the Sunset Riots, and even the armed security which gripped Woodland Meadows before my takeover. Although historically not progressive, the CPD determined that respecting the citizenry was more effective than beating them.

On Oct. 8th, over a thousand supporters of all ages, races, and backgrounds marched through the streets of Cincinnati and massed at the end with a rally in Fountain Square. A variety of speakers and musicians participated and the event was successful in bringing together supporters and exchanging ideas. The police monitored, but did not threaten. Our permit expired at one in the morning. Many had left, but an Occupation was planned, so I joined about 50 others who sat down in the square. The police were aware that an occupation was contemplated, and had warned that arrests would follow. We didn't know how many were willing to be taken into custody.

After about an hour, the police advised that anyone who did not want to get arrested should move to the sidewalk. I recalled being in custody in Beaumont, but thankfully, I never saw the inside of a jail cell. And I didn't want to. I got up, along with the majority of the others. However, 10 remained seated, ready to go to jail for the cause, prepared to enter a burn zone. The rest of us regrouped on the sidewalk. An anticipatory silence electrified the air. I thought back to the 2,500 punks sitting down at the T.S.O.L. concert almost three decades earlier. The unease escalated as a CPD paddy wagon appeared and multiple officers surrounded the square with sets of plastic handcuffs in their hands. Was this going to be another Sunset Riot?

On the sidewalk, maybe 40 of us marched back and forth, chanting, "Banks got bailed out! We got sold out!" and other Occupy anthems. Some patrons of nearby hotels complained to the police, who asked us to reduce the volume. We did. The uncertainty, tension, and energy were fusing into an early morning that felt surreal and, at least for Cincinnati, historic. No one knew what would happen. As the hours ticked by, the 10 sat in the center of the square, the 40 continued to chant, and the police stood at the ready with their plastic handcuffs.

I thought back to my father's arrest and beating by police in Argentina. At the time, Argentine leaders had, according to Wikipedia, "began a policy of liberal economic moves that mostly benefitted the nation's upper classes and permitted great political and industrial corruption at the expense of national growth." Seventy years ago, my father was arrested for standing up against the same injustices we were protesting tonight. I realized that maybe we were on the doorstep of change. I felt a jolt of adrenaline and optimism, a sensation I had not felt since my runs through pre-storm Woodland Meadows.

What happened next was unanticipated. As we neared the 6:00 AM re-opening time for the square, none of the 10 had been arrested—they were still there, seated. As the clock wound down, all of us on the sidewalk counted down each second of the final minute and then spontaneously rushed onto the square to reconnect with the 10. We were cheering, for the 10 and for ourselves, for the city and even for the CPD. Everyone won that day.

I can only speculate that the lack of arrests was a nod to Occupy Cincinnati for the proactive dialogue with CPD that preceded the event. If so, this exemplified diplomatic policing which other departments should emulate.

To occupy Fountain Square would have displaced many upcoming events. Thus, the occupation moved a short distance to Piatt Park, nestled in a large median that housed the movement for several weeks. I had lit the match, but could not contribute much more, as I was preparing to move AHP to Chicago at the end of October. Yet, I stayed in contact with several friends I gained in these few weeks. Unfortunately, the elite soon cut the Occupy movements across the country short.

As Occupy grew to epic size, the FBI, Department of Homeland Security, local police, and big banks coordinated a nationwide crackdown, according to documents produced in response to a Freedom of Information Act request. Mara Verheyden-Hilliard, executive director of the Partnership for Civil Justice Fund explained:

> *"These documents show that the FBI and the Department of Homeland Security are treating protests against the corporate and banking structure of America as potential criminal and terrorist activity. These documents also show these federal agencies functioning as a de facto intelligence arm of Wall Street and Corporate America."*

The Guardian wrote that:

> *"The crackdown, which involved...violent arrests, group disruption, canister missiles to the skulls of protesters, people held in handcuffs so tight they were injured, people held in bondage till they were forced to wet or soil themselves—was coordinated with the big banks themselves."*

However, many of the rich were also upset with the direction of our country and came out to join Occupy. Some celebrity elites who supported Occupy include Yoko Ono, Russell Simmons, Roseanne Barr, Deepak Chopra, Kanye West, Alec Baldwin, Susan Sarandon, Michael Moore, and Tim Robbins. Sadly, some Occupy members derided the involvement of some elites and,

Nine of the 10 remaining protestors on Fountain Square (Photo: © David Sorcher 2011)

notably, Michael Moore was particularly slammed in an unfortunate manner. A handful of Occupiers jeered him due to his wealth as he spoke at an Occupy Wall Street gathering.

Moore earned his money without enslaving people—we all had a choice as to whether to spend our dollars to buy tickets to his movies. His movies were enlightening and entertaining. I saw *Farenheit 911* and *Sicko* with my dad, who was a big Moore fan. We were happy to pay for the tickets, and we did not leave the theater with burdens on our backs.

I want to realize the vision my father dreamed of over 70 years ago, my punk friends and I envisioned 30 years ago, and Anonymous and Occupy seek now: a better country for all. In order to change this country, we need the support of everyone who shares our mission, whether they are rich or poor.

CHAPTER EIGHT

What Is Peace, but Love?

"VERRIA, WILL YOU MARRY ME?" I WAS ON MY KNEE IN THE kitchen of our Chicago apartment on the chilly evening of Jan. 6, 2012. I had been carrying around the engagement ring, which I purchased used on eBay, since mid-December.

The down payment for a new ring would have been $700, followed by three years of monthly payments. Instead, I paid $700 for a ring that would have sold new for four times that. It was an easy decision, and the ring was beautiful: white gold with some modest-sized sparklers. No huge rock, but that wouldn't be Verria or me. I knew she would like it and, more importantly, what this meant for us. However, once it arrived I had difficulty presenting it to her.

I planned to ask Verria to marry me surrounded by friends and family when we celebrated Christmas in Los Angeles, but I hesitated. Although American Homeowner Preservation was growing, I was financially much worse off than I was a decade earlier, before my Woodland Meadows catastrophe. A part of me yearned to regain the ground I had lost, and perceived marriage as a distraction from this quest. The ring stayed in my pocket through the holiday.

After Los Angeles, we had gone to San Francisco to celebrate New Year's Day. As we walked around a local lake on the first day of 2012, the crisp air swirled with hope and promise. *"Now is the time,"* I had thought to myself. Still, I could not bring myself to ask.

Finally, the moment had come. "Yes, of course, but are you sure?" responded Verria, happy but guarded. We had been together for six years and I had gotten uncomfortable every time the topic of marriage came up. I was 46 and Verria was 43. Neither of us had ever married.

"Yes, I am sure," I said, pleased that I finally took the step, which was easier than I had imagined once I finally did it. I got up and we held each other tightly. When I was born in 1965, a white/ Hispanic man marrying a black woman was a felony in some parts of America. The Georgia Supreme Court ruled in 1869 that:

> *"...moral or social equality between the different races...does not in fact exist, and never can. The God of nature made it otherwise, and no human law can produce it, and no human tribunal can enforce it. There are gradations and classes throughout the universe. From the tallest archangel in Heaven, down to the meanest reptile on earth, moral and social inequalities exist, and must continue to exist throughout all eternity."*

"Just to be certain, I am not going to tell anyone for two weeks," Verria said. In 1967, 16 states still had laws outlawing interracial marriage. That same year, the Supreme Court legalized interracial unions nationwide in *Loving v. Virginia*. Something had changed. This case has been regularly cited in the recent efforts to legalize same-sex marriage. Something is changing. If anyone had a problem with Verria and I mixing the races, they either kept it to themselves or I didn't notice.

"I'm not going to change my mind," I said. Still, I honored her request. Our marriage would be a fitting exit from my Woodland Meadows' burn zone. In my mind, when I survived a burn zone, there was a reward for my sacrifice. I had survived Woodland Meadows and expected my eventual prize to be a return of my financial losses. This had not happened, but maybe my reward was something better. I needed to allow myself to be happy.

"Okay. I love you," she said.

"Dad, we are getting married," I said to my father by phone after two weeks had passed. By this time, my father's cancer had worsened and he was living in a rehab center in Santa Monica, Calif.

"Congratulations, Jorgie," he said. Both my parents liked Verria and I believe they were happy if I was happy. "When will you have the wedding?"

"I want to have it in June in the garden at Homedale," I said. "Homedale" referred to Homedale Street, where my parents had owned their home since 1965, the year I was born. Although my dad had been spending most of his time at rehab centers, my mum still lived there. I wanted my parents involved in the planning and I knew they would want to do all they could to make the day special.

"Wonderful. I will plan the layout of the tables and chairs," my father said. "And we must open a sliding glass door from the living room to the garden." In the subsequent months, my father went about designing from his hospital bed, with occasional visits to Homedale to take measurements and check progress. His cancer continued to debilitate him, but the wedding preparations gave him purpose and focus. What had started out as dark blotches on his skin now looked like black and bloody plums protruding from his legs. As nurses wrapped his bandages tightly to constrain the oozy emissions, he sketched where the wedding tables and decorations would be laid out around the garden.

"Where is everyone?" asked my bride on our wedding day, June 16, 2012. We were surveying the many empty chairs set out for our guests at Homedale. "The ceremony is supposed to start in 15 minutes."

"I am sure that they are all on their way," I said, feeling a bit anxious myself. Luckily, I had run 16 miles that morning with some old friends, so my nerves were calmed. Still, more than half the guests had not arrived.

"Are you sure that they all confirmed?" I asked.

"Yes, they all confirmed. What is going on?" asked my wife, who was getting made up while I was running, so her nerves were starting to fray.

"We'll be fine, we're the only two who really have to be here," I said, trying to sound reassuring. Then, my cell phone started ringing.

"Jorgie," said my cousin Santiago, sounding a tad anxious. "We are on the freeway and the traffic is horrid. Bumper-to-bumper. We heard on the radio that UCLA graduation is this afternoon as well."

"Okay, just get here as fast as you can," I said.

"Verria, it's the traffic. The UCLA graduation is going on this afternoon," I said. "Let's just wait." At just after 3:00 PM, more than an hour later, most of the guests had arrived. Verria, looking magnificent, prepared to walk down the aisle. Soon, the minister, a friend of Verria's, began the ceremony:

"In their years together, each one has been through some significant personal challenges. They've each had their turn to see how the other was always there to support them as well as to discover how well each navigated his or her challenging terrain. The result of those times, fortunately now relegated to the past, is mutual respect and admiration as well as the unshakeable confidence that they can depend on one another. And it is with this certainty that they enter the sacred sacrament and commitment of marriage and life-long partnership. And, while perhaps not starry-eyed, they also bring passion, joy, shared interests, and absolute trust to their nuptials."

I gazed into Verria's eyes as the minister said these words. I clasped her hands. We were standing in front of the sliding glass doors, which my dad's vision had turned into a splendid reality. I glanced at my father in his wheelchair and my mother at his side. I felt calm and at peace, in the presence of those closest to me. I no longer felt like a loner, not so much at least. I felt loved and in love.

I closed my eyes. Within 50 feet of where I stood, my parents had read me bedtime stories; my brothers and I spent hours watching *Scooby Doo* and other cartoons; I wrapped newspapers in rubber bands as I prepared for my route; I hurriedly unloaded ice cream treats from my dad's Squareback into the freezer; I first played *London Calling* on my turntable; I asked my parents to let me leave high school at 16; punk icons had spent the night in sleeping bags; I first shaved my legs as I resolved to become a bike racer; and I dressed in my Brooks Brothers suit, with my dad tying my tie, readying for my interview with Mike Dodd. This was the right place for the second half of my life to begin.

> *"Let us also acknowledge and, in a sense, invoke the presence of a few other people who are unable to be here at least physically—to share in this ceremony and celebration. These are family members who mean so much to the bride and groom. Verria told me that her mother was, without a doubt, her best friend and that she knows her mother is smiling down upon her."*

As I looked into Verria's eyes, I saw tears appear.

> *"Likewise, if Verria's father were able to be here, he would be adding his own blessings in person. And though, due to certain challenges, he just couldn't make it happen, we*

know in his heart, he is present. So as we look around this room at each one of you who has, in some way, helped shape this couple into who is standing so beautifully before us, we also want to honor Verria's parents' contributions as well, inviting them both to be here through the bonds of love that somehow transcend the constraints of time, distance, dimension, and struggle."

By now, Verria was crying, as were most of the guests, and me. The tears were contagious.

"At this time, I am very pleased to call upon Jorge's mother, Jennifer Newbery, to offer a reading to her son and soon-to-be daughter-in-law."

"This is a passage from a book by my mother, Peggy," my mother said, before she broke down into sobs, catching the crying contagion that had swept the ceremony. I perceived that her tears were a reaction to the emotions swirling in her mind: sadness at the early passing of Verria's mother, happiness for our nuptials, the memories of her mother, and her pending presentation.

"Maybe she doesn't have to read?" asked my brother Charles.

"I want to. I will be fine," said my mother, recovering. By now, everyone present was weeping. However, my mother was entering a burn zone. She had practiced these words for months. She knew she could do this. She would be challenged for a period, but she summoned the conviction and power of her years on the stage. She delivered her lines:

The mind drawn up to hopes, not fears, and wishes
As gently as the coolly falling dew.
No thing was great
But beauty, gentleness, and heritage,
And music, spiring with its silver sound
To cure the intricate heart. No thing was true
But goodness. And no dream was true
But the good dream.

I imagined my mother on the stage when she was 16 as the half-caste Tondelayo in *White Cargo*. Her voice was as powerful and mesmerizing now as it was then. Her effort was bearing fruit. *"Keep going Mum, you're doing great,"* I thought.

Perhaps some loss to come
Had brought the quiet where the simple days
Allot the theme.
And where the dreams of empires, grandeurs
Are little things. And only lover's arms
Embrace the world.
...the love of Man for man,
of God, for man,
Of God, by man
That is the important thing.

As my mother spoke with strength, the ceremony was engulfed in tears flowing from everyone present. Still, she continued unwaveringly, drawing on her actor's skills to block out distractions.

Or some fulfillment
Gone at its perfect chord
Yet gentle, true
So that the chord rings in the heart forever,
Never to be forgotten, never stilled:
The perfect harmony that tunes the soul
To some deep peace, and vibrant, so that days
Are changed. And life is changed. 'For
these attract the soul'
The marvelous, enameled, and glissading hours
Of the perfection, answered.
What is peace,
But love?

"My mother signed the book, 'To Jenny, may your star shine bright,'" my mum said. "And that's what I wish for Jorge and Verria: May your star shine bright."

As she spoke the final word, she exited the burn zone, her reward bestowed: my mother's words were her wedding present to us, and they meant more than any material gift. Tears were escaping out of my eyes, even though I tried to stifle them. I felt gratitude and awe for my mother and all that she had shared with me. I wanted an encore performance, but first, I had a recital of my own.

"I, Jorge, take you, Verria, to be my lawfully wedded wife,
my constant friend, my faithful partner and my love from
this day forward," I said. "In the presence of our family and
friends, I offer you my solemn vow to be your faithful partner
in sickness and in health, in good times and in bad, in joy

as well as in sorrow. I promise to love you unconditionally, to support you in your goals, to honor and respect you, to laugh with you and cry with you, and to cherish you for as long as we both shall live."

As the ceremony wound down, my anxiety level rose. This was my wedding, so I would have to dance, just Verria and me. There was no swirling mosh pit here for me to jump into.

I put my arms around Verria's waist, and her hands clasped around my neck. I held her close and we started to sway side to side, the one dance step I have mastered. "That went well," I said as I looked into Verria's eyes.

"Yes, it did," she said.

My bride and I with my parents, prior to the tear-jerking ceremony

Don't let this photo fool you: my musical talents remained as feeble as my dance moves. I was just pretending I could play the piano.

CHAPTER NINE

Time Strokes the Chord

"MUM, CAN I BORROW YOUR MOTHER'S BOOK?" I ASKED ON my next trip back to Los Angeles, for my father's 92nd birthday in July 2012. "I would like to read more." By now, my father's condition was getting severe. I drove him from the rehab center to Homedale for a celebratory dinner. After our guests had left and my mother and sisters were cleaning up in the kitchen, my father shared words a child does not want to hear.

"Jorgie, I want to ask you something," my dad said calmly, but intently. "I want to be cremated and laid to rest next to my parents in La Recoleta." This was the Newbery tomb in Argentina which we had visited 20 years prior.

"Dad..." I didn't know what to say. I didn't want him thinking about death.

"I want you to take me to Argentina," he asked. He was so frail now. I didn't know how this was going to happen. "I want to say goodbye to everyone there, then remain. I am going to ask Charles if I can stay with him."

"Have you talked with Mum?" I asked.

"Not yet, but she'll understand. She will want to stay here with Anne and be nearer to all of you," he said. "Anne has helped us both, and now she can keep helping your mother." My mother was 87 and had health challenges of her own.

"I will take you," I said. "Do your doctors think it's okay?"

"They thought I'd die years ago," he said.

"Alright, you just need to gain some strength," I said.

We soon agreed to travel over Thanksgiving. Over the next few months, my father proudly shared news of his regular exercise classes and physical therapy. He was preparing for this flight as he had trained for his many marathons of decades past. He had purpose yet again, another challenge to surmount. I waited until two weeks before the trip to buy the plane tickets, still not completely convinced that he would be ready for the 16 hours of air travel.

"I feel strong, Jorgie," my father said. "The doctor says I need to get up and walk up and down the aisle every hour and hang onto to the seatbacks for support." I knew my dad wanted to return to Argentina, and he had readied himself well. All I could do was to support his wish, regardless of his condition. I bought the tickets.

On the Saturday before Thanksgiving 2012, I pulled up my rental car into the alley behind the rehab center in Santa Monica where my dad had lived for several months.

"We're going," I said, recalling our first trip together to Argentina 20 years prior. Back then, he returned to say hello to all his friends and family there. That was his first return to Argentina in 40 years. I shuddered with melancholy for a moment as I realized that this would be his final return, and now he was going to say goodbye to all his friends and family permanently.

"I'm ready, Jorgie," he said. His face had sunk and his skin was ashen. Still, his smile glowed and his eyes gleamed. He was eager to enter his burn zone. My father executed his plan on the plane: He diligently arose every hour to walk up and down the aisle, plus performed some hand clapping exercises to keep his circulation up. The bandages on his legs became soaked with blood and other cancer-induced discharges as time passed. He was in a burn zone, but he was in control and knew that the effort would subside once we landed. I stayed awake almost the whole flight, watching out for my dad. My brother Charles was waiting in Argentina with a nurse to attend to my father once we arrived. My job was simply to get him there safely. Mission accomplished.

The next day, my father was on the phone, calling friends, announcing his successful arrival. Several made plans to visit him. In the afternoon, he asked me to take him for a walk. I pushed him in his wheelchair out to the front sidewalk.

"I need to get stronger. I don't want the wheelchair," he said. "I can do this myself. I am going to go around the block. I want you to come with me." I helped him out of his wheelchair and up to standing. My father started walking with his walker. He moved very slowly, and I followed closely behind to catch him in case he fell. We left the wheelchair behind in front of Charles and Jenny's house.

"You're doing great," I said encouragingly. Although his pace was leaden, I recognized the enormous effort he was exerting. Once again, my father had entered a self-inflicted burn zone to challenge his 92-year-old cancer-riddled body and test his limits. His mission: walk around a city block. His reward: accomplish a goal, and maybe the ability to set a greater objective for tomorrow.

"I need to rest," he said. We had gone about halfway. I helped him onto a bus bench. He looked exhausted.

"Dad, you did great just getting here. Yesterday, you made the whole plane trip. Now, you have walked halfway around the block," I said. "You are doing great."

"I want to keep going," he said.

"I know you do," I said. We sat silently for several minutes. I think he was too tired to even talk. We enjoyed the view of this potholed street in my father's homeland, which he had left 60 years ago in search of a better life in America.

"Do you want me to go back to get the wheelchair?" I finally asked.

"Okay," he said. I ran back, suddenly realizing that I had left the wheelchair on the sidewalk. I had anticipated that we would be back much sooner. However, as I arrived, I could not see the wheelchair.

"You fucking idiot," my sister-in-law Jenny said, as I entered the house. Thankfully, I found that someone, probably Jenny, had moved the wheelchair inside. I knew why she was upset and I didn't engage her. Both of my brothers and my sisters-in-law believed that my father should slow down and stop taking risks. He certainly should not be trying to walk the rutted sidewalk around the block. This was perceived as precarious and risky. With the wheelchair in front of me, I ran back to my dad. Maybe 10 minutes had passed.

"Dad, are you okay?" I said as I returned. He had nodded off to sleep, sitting on the bench. I tapped his shoulder. A sudden scare roiled through me. I then shook his shoulder. "Dad, are you okay?"

"Yes," he awoke, startled. "Yes, Jorgie, I am okay." I helped him into the wheelchair and pushed him home.

When I left for the U.S. on the Saturday after Thanksgiving, I gave my father a hug and a kiss. "I love you." I wasn't sure if I would ever see him again.

My dad with my brother Charles and grandchildren Jasper, Chloe and Saffron, 2013

Over the subsequent months, my father spoke happily by phone of attending the school events of Charles and Jenny's children, his three grandchildren. He would take his walker most mornings to get coffee and read the newspaper at a nearby café. He was clinging to his independence, often ignoring the nurse who visited frequently to assist him.

"He has fallen twice and has trouble walking," Charles said by phone in May 2013. "He has not been out of bed in two weeks." I had noticed that even minor injuries seemed to take longer and longer to recover from as my parents aged. Charles handed the phone to my dad.

"Dad, how are you?" I asked.

"I want to get out of bed, but the doctor say it's too dangerous," he said. "They say I should just stay in bed, but I don't feel good staying in bed. I think I am getting worse." I thought of America and all the tens of millions of families who know something is wrong with unaffordable debt and an ever-widening wealth gap. *"But to do something is risky. Look at Occupy, Anonymous, the punks. They got beaten or arrested,"* people may think. Sometimes taking action includes uncertainty, the risk of failure. Sometimes when you enter a burn zone, you don't know whether you will emerge.

"Dad, I want to come and see you," I said.

"OK, Jorgie" he said. "I would like that." A few weeks later, when I arrived, my father was in good spirits, but bedridden. My brother, sister-in-law, and the doctors were all singing the same tune: "He must stay in bed. Walking is too perilous." His muscles were atrophying and his strength dissipating. He would do exercises in bed where he would rotate his feet and clap his hands to spur blood flow. But these did little to decelerate his body's deterioration. The bloody plums on his legs now looked more like smashed pumpkins embedded in his skin, which was cracking and bleeding.

"What does he have to lose?" I pleaded. "If he falls again, he will be back in bed. Even if he dies, he will die living the life he wants. That should be his choice."

"The risk is too great," the doctor said.

"The risk of what?" I countered. "What are you trying to protect him from? He's 92-years-old and has had stage 3 cancer for years."

"Dad, do you want to come to live with me in Chicago?" I asked, as I sat at my father's bedside. As soon as I said it, I realized that this was impractical and that my dad wanted to take his last breath in Argentina. Still, something had to change. He needed to be allowed to walk and try to improve himself. He was wasting away.

"*Something has to change,*" I thought. My father was miserable. The words of anthropologist and author Margaret Mead swam through my brain: "Never believe that a few caring people can't change the world. For, indeed, that's all who ever have."

"I would love to be with you," he said. "But I need to stay in Argentina." A few days later, I said goodbye to my father before I headed to the airport to return to the U.S.

"Bye, Daddy," I said. "I love you."

"I love you, Jorgie," he said.

On the flight home, I finally opened up the *The Democrat's Chapbook* by my grandmother, Peggy Whitehouse, whose words my mother shared at my wedding. My grandmother was an authoress in England who lived through both World Wars. I never met her. As I read, her writings exposed wrongs and advocated for the oppressed. "*That's what I want to do,*" I thought. She wrote these words in the midst of World War II in 1942:

We have not known democracy, only
  license, fear and wildness,
Not taking any responsibility in our government
  or having any feeling of it.
Like Plato's Democrat, the all-for-nothing rebel,
Our great experiment has kicked our
  people to mere gutter-rags.

My grandmother's words haunted my brain. She was witness to the same injustice in 1942 in the U.K. as we had today in the U.S. There had to be a metamorphosis, but simply shining a light on the difficulties did not appear to be a sufficient catalyst. Something had to change.

"Jorgie, I cannot hang on much longer. The pain is too much," my father said on Sep. 14, 2013. He sounded purposeful and determined—not sad, but tired. He had realized that he wasn't going to exit his final burn zone. He was calling to say goodbye. "I have always loved you."

"I love you, too," I said, chokingly.

"Please take care of the family," he asked.

"I will," I said, as my eyes welled up. My father called my mother and each of his children that day to say goodbye.

"He spent most of yesterday with the priest," Charles shared. "He seems at peace." That night, he told Charles that he was ready for death. Once again, my grandmother's words sounded in my mind:

The answer to this does not lie in the system
But in re-education, of ourselves.

I called my father every day for the next eight days, after his goodbye call. Oftentimes, he was too weak to talk. However, I did get through one day when my cousin Barbara had visited and was cooking lunch.

"What is cooking?" asked my father, perking up, as I was on the line.

"Fish pie," I heard someone reply.

"Barbara is cooking that wonderful fish pie," he said, sounding quite happy. I found this encouraging. An appetite is a sign of being alive, and wanting to live.

Time strokes the chord.
Resolved to a harmony I hear the discords cease.
The harpist time
Strikes now.

"Hi Jorge," Charles said by early-morning phone call. I was already in the office, seated at my desk, and no one else was in yet. I could tell by his tone that this was the call I was dreading. The day was Sep. 23, 2013.

"No," I said. I felt asphyxiated, like the day Trudy Bartley said, "We're going to shut down Woodland Meadows." But this was 10 times worse. There was no hope to reverse this.

"Yes, he passed last night in his sleep," Charles said.

"Okay, thanks for calling and helping him out so much, to Jenny too," I said, haltingly. I hung up and let out a wail that I had never experienced before in my life.

Visions of my father blurred through my mind: running together as a child, driving me to get ice cream, dropping me off at the Whisky-A-Go-Go, the Sunset Riots, the bike races, selecting my first suit at Brooks Brothers, on our trips to Argentina, at all the birthday dinners, planning the wedding, sitting together on that bus bench in Argentina. A piece of me was gone. However, I reasoned that a piece of my father was left behind: me.

My father spent his life challenging himself, exploring his limits, taking risks, stepping out of his comfort zone, and willingly jumping into burn zones. He did not do this haphazardly. Instead, he prepared for his trials. He never taught me to do the same. Instead, he lived his life and set an example for me to follow. I thank him for that.

CHAPTER TEN

Take Control

MY WIFE AND I WERE WALKING TO WORK ON A PLEASANT
October morning in 2014. We don't own a car as we live and
work in downtown Chicago. The distance between our apartment and AHP's office is about six long blocks. As we walked, she
scanned emails on her smartphone. I had been up late writing
this book, and Woodland Meadows was on my brain all night
as I slept. My mind was racing. Suddenly, I solved a riddle.

"I am the magic bullet," I said, out loud. We were walking east
on Roosevelt Road when we got stopped at the traffic light at
Clark, just outside the Target store.

"You are a bullet?" my wife asked, perplexed. She put down her
smartphone as we jaywalked through the red, a very common
crime in Chicago.

"I just realized that I am the magic bullet," I said. "When

Woodland Meadows spun out of control, I was always searching for a quick fix to turn my predicament around. I was paying tons of money to attorneys and lobbyists."

"But none of those guys got any results," she said.

"Exactly. I kept searching for the magic bullet," I said. "I was buying lottery tickets, *real* lottery tickets. Paying these guys was the exact same thing. I kept hoping that one of them would be the cure-all for my chaos."

"You bought lottery tickets?" she asked. "You never do that."

"I know. I never gamble," I said. "But back then, I was buying scratchers, playing the lotto numbers on Saturday nights. I even bought a book about picking the best lottery numbers."

"Did you win anything?" she asked.

"Once in a while, I'd win a free ticket or $5, but I'd just blow that on more tickets," I said. "Just like the attorneys and lobbyists. I kept putting more money in their pockets, but nothing came back." We were now moving north on State Street, past FFC, the gym where we both work out.

"You spent hundreds of thousands," she said. "All wasted. Nothing to show for it."

"I was searching for the magic bullet," I said. "In the end, though, the only one who actually did anything for me was *me*. My magic bullet was not some external person or force. It was me."

"Okay, honey," she said, gently. "You are my magic bullet."

"Not exactly," I replied. "I am my magic bullet. You are your magic bullet. The decisions that led to my Woodland Meadows meltdown were mine. No one forced me to buy Woodland Meadows. I could have closed it down right after the storm. I could have hired another contractor besides philandering Belfor. I could have made any number of other decisions which could have resulted in a better outcome."

"Hindsight is 20/20. Don't beat yourself up," said my wife.

"I am not beating myself up. I am just trying to reckon in my mind with what happened," I said. "I could blame all my woes on the city and, sure, they do have some culpability. In the end, though, the decisions that ended up unraveling my life were mine alone."

"But you built yourself back up," she said. We had arrived and were now alone in the elevator going to the sixth floor.

"Exactly, I built myself back up," I said. "I had to do it. No one else could do it."

"I think I helped," she said. I unlocked the door to suite 606, AHP's offices.

"Yes, you helped and supported me and I love you for that," I said. "But your help and support would have had no impact if I didn't lift myself up in the first place. I control myself and no one else does. If I got myself into trouble, I needed to get myself out. No one else was going to do that for me."

As I settled in at my desk, I leaned back in my chair and stared at the ceiling. I thought of all the thousands of families whose mortgages AHP now owns. Engulfed in burn zones, some ignore our outreach efforts. AHP can help, but each debtor is their own magic bullet. We cannot solve their problems for them. They need to want our help. *"Stay relaxed,"* I wanted to counsel them. *"Others around you are hurting just as much as you. Focus on enduring the pain until the pace slows. The effort will get easier soon."* I wanted every one of them to know what happened to me.

My experiences have not all been happy, and certainly my challenges have at times created strife for me. I learned to play life's bad hands and I have shared my story with you in this book. If you have burn zones that you think you cannot withstand, debts that you cannot afford, or hurdles you believe you cannot overcome, prepare to test the limits of your body and mind. Get ready to enter your burn zone.

About the Author

JORGE P. NEWBERY IS A SUCCESSFUL entrepreneur, distressed debt and real estate investor, endurance athlete, and author.

He turned around some of the country's most troubled housing complexes in amassing a portfolio of 4,000 apartments across the USA  1992–2005. However, a natural disaster triggered a financial collapse in which he lost everything and emerged over $26 million in debt. He never filed bankruptcy, instead developing strategies to gain leverage over creditors and settle debts at huge discounts, or simply not pay them at all. He is a veteran of dozens of court battles, once fighting a creditor to the Missouri Court of Appeals, which found that "the entire debt was inadvertently extinguished" by sloppy legal work. The debt was over $5,800,000!

Today, Newbery helps others crushed by unaffordable debts rebuild their lives. He is founder and CEO of American Homeowner Preservation, a socially responsible hedge fund which purchases nonperforming mortgages from banks at big discounts, then shares the discounts with families to settle their mortgages at terms many borrowers find "too good to be true."

He is the author of the autobiographical *Burn Zones: Playing Life's Bad Hands* and the upcoming *Debt Cleanse: How To Settle Your Debts For Pennies On The Dollar (And Not Pay Some At All)*. He regularly contributes to Huffington Post and other publications, plus speaks regularly on debt, investing, finance and housing issues.

Newbery raced bicycles for a living from 1986–1990 as a Category 1. He competed in the 1988 Olympic Trials and was 4th in the Spenco 500, a nonstop 500-mile bike race televised on ESPN. He also raced for the Costa Rican National Team in the Tour of Mexico, was 2nd in the 1987 Southern California State Championship Road Race, plus held the Green Jersey in the 1987 Vulcan Tour. Today, Newbery runs and has completed over 70 marathons and ultra marathons. In 2012, he was the overall winner of the Chicago Lakefront 50K. At 46-years-old, he was nearly double the age of the 24-year-old second-place finisher.

Find him on Twitter @JorgePNewbery

Made in the USA
Coppell, TX
28 September 2020